John Flavel

Navigation Spiritualized

A New Compass for Seamen

John Flavel

Navigation Spiritualized
A New Compass for Seamen

ISBN/EAN: 9783337336608

Printed in Europe, USA, Canada, Australia, Japan

Cover: Foto ©ninafisch / pixelio.de

More available books at **www.hansebooks.com**

SPIRITUALIZED;

OR A

NEW COMPASS

FOR

SEAMEN,

CONSISTING OF XXXII *POINTS*;

OF { PLEASANT OBSERVATIONS,
PROFITABLE APPLICATIONS,
and SERIOUS REFLECTIONS,

ALL CONCLUDED WITH SO MANY
SPIRITUAL POEMS.

BY *JOHN FLAVEL,*

MINISTER OF THE GOSPEL AT DARTMOUTH IN ENGLAND.

PRINTED BY
EDMUND M. BLUNT,
AT THE NEWBURYPORT BOOK-STORE,
1796.

NAVIGATION

SPIRITUALIZED

OR

A NEW COMPASS FOR SEAMEN,

Confisting of XXXII POINTS;

Of {PLEASANT OBSERVATIONS, PROFITABLE APPLICATIONS, and SERIOUS REFLECTIONS.

All to conclude with so many Spiritual POEMS.

What good might seamen get, if once they were
But heavenly minded ? If they could but steer
The christian's course, the soul might then enjoy
Sweet peace, they might like seas o'erflow with joy.
Were God, our all, how would our comforts double
Upon us ! thus the seas of all our trouble
Would be divinely sweet : men should endeavour
To see God now, and be with him forever.

TO ALL

Masters, Mariners, and Seamen.

SIRS,

I FIND it storyed of *Anacharsis*, that when one asked him, whether the living or the dead were more ? He returned this answer, *You must first tell me* (faith he) *in which number I must place seamen*; intimating thereby, that seamen are as it were, a third sort of persons, to be numbered neither with the living nor the dead; their lives hanging continually in suspence before them. And it was anciently accounted the most desperate employment, and they little better than lost men that used the seas. "Through all my life *(faith Aristotle)* three things do especially repent me: First, That ever I revealed a secret to a woman. Secondly, That ever I remained one day without a will. Thirdly, That ever I went to any place by sea, whether I might have gone by land. Nothing *(faith another)* is more miserable, than to see a virtuous and worthy person upon the sea." And although custom, and the great improvement of the art of navigation, have made it less formidable now, yet you are no further from death than you are from the waters, which is but a remove of two or three inches. Now you that border so nigh upon the confines of death and eternity every moment, may well be supposed to be men of singular piety and serious: for nothing composes the heart more to such a frame, than the lively apprehensions of eternity do: and none have greater external advantages for that, than you have. But alas! for the generality, What sort of men are more ungodly, and stupidly insensible of eternal concernments? Living for the most part, as if they had made a covenant with death, and with hell were at an agreement. It was an ancient saying, "Qui nescit orare, discat navigare." He that knows not how to pray, let him go to sea. But we may say now, (alas, that we may say so in times of greater light) He that would learn to be profane, to drink, and swear, and dishonour God, let him go to sea. As for prayer, it is a rare thing among seamen, they count that a needless business: they see the prophane and vile delivered as well as others; and therefore, What profit is there if they pray unto him? Mal. 3. 4. As I remember, I have read of a profane soldier, who was heard swearing, though he stood in a place of great danger; and when one that stood by him warned him, saying, "Fellow-soldier, do not swear, the bullets flie;" he answered "They that swear come off as well as they that pray." Soon after a shot hit him and down he fell. Plato diligently admonished all men to avoid the sea; "For (saith he) it is the school-master of all vice and dishonesty." Sirs! it is a very sad consideration to me, that you who float upon the great deeps, in whose bottom so many thousand poor miserable creatures lie, whose sins have sunk them down not only into the bottom of the sea, but of hell also, whither divine vengeance hath pursued them: That you (I say) who daily float, and hover over them, and have the roaring waves and billows that swallowed them up, gaping for you at the next prey, should be no more affected with these things. Oh what a terrible voice doth God utter in the storms! "It breaks the ceders, shakes the wilderness, makes the hinds to calve," Psa. xxix. 5. And can it not shake your hearts. This voice of the Lord is full of majesty, but his voice in the word is more efficacious and powerful, Heb. iv. 12. To convince and rip up the heart. This word is exalted above all his name. Psa. cxxxviii. 3. And if it cannot awaken you, it is no wonder you remain secure and dead, when the Lord utters his voice in the most dreadful storms and tempests. But if neither the voice of God uttered in his dreadful works, or in his glorious gospel, can effectually awaken and rouze, there is an *Euroclidon*, a fearful storm coming, which will so awaken your souls, as that they shall never sleep any more. Psa. xii. 6. " Upon the wicked he shall rain snares, fire and brimstone, and an horrible tempest: This is the portion of their cup." You that have been at sea in the most violent storms, never felt such a storm as this, and the Lord grant you never may; no calm shall follow this storm. There are some among you, that, I am persuaded, do truly fear that God in whose hand their life and breath is: Men that fear an oath, and are an honour to their profession; who drive a trade for *heaven*, and are diligent to secure the happiness of their immortal souls, in the insurance-office above: but for the generality, alas! they mind none of these things. How many of you are coasting to and fro, from one country to another? But never think of that *heavenly* country above, nor how you may get the merchandize thereof, which is better than the gold of *Ophir*. How oft do you tremble to see the foaming waves dance about you, and wash over you? yet consider not how terrible it will be to have all the waves and billows of God's wrath to go over your souls, and that for ever. How glad are you, after you have been long tossed upon the ocean, to descry land. And how yare and eagerly do you look out for it? Who yet never had your hearts warmed with the consideration of that joy which shall be among the *saints*, when they arrive at the *heavenly strand*, and set foot on the shore of glory.

O Sirs! I beg of you, if you have any regard to those precious immortal souls of yours, which are also imbarqued for *eternity*, whether all winds blow them, and will quickly be at their port of heaven or hell, that you will seriously mind these things, and learn to steer your course to heaven, and improve all winds (I mean opportunities and means) to waft you thither.

Here you venture life and liberty, run through many difficulties and dangers, and all to compass a perishing treasure; yet how often do you return disappointed in your designs? Or if not, yet it is but a fading short-lived inheritance, which like the flowing tide, for a little while, covers the shore, and then returns, and leaves it naked and dry again: And are not everlasting treasures worth venturing for? Good souls, be wise for eternity: I here present you with the fruit of a few spare hours, redeemed for your sakes, from my other studies and employments, which I have put into a new dress and mode. I have endeavoured to clothe spiritual matters in your own dialect and phrases, that they might be the more intelligible to you; and added some pious poems, with which the several chapters are concluded, trying by all means to assault your several affections, and as the Apostle speaks, *to catch you with guile*. I can say nothing of it; I know it cannot be without its manifold imperfections, since I am conscious of so many in myself: Only this I will adventure to say of it, That how defective or empty soever it be in other respects, yet it is stuffed and filled with much true love to, and earnest desires after the salvation and prosperity of your souls. And for the other defects that attend it, I have only two things to offer, in way of excuse: It is the first essay that ever I made in this kind, wherein I had no precedent: And it was hastened, for your sakes, too soon out of my hands, that it might be ready to wait upon you, when you undertake your next voyage; so that I could not revise and polish it. Nor indeed was I sollicitous above the ſtile, I conſider, I write not for critical and learned perſons: My deſign is not to pleaſe your fancies any further than I might thereby get any advantage to profit your ſouls. I will not once queſtion your welcome reception of it: If God ſhall bleſs theſe meditations to the converſion of any one among you, you will be the gainers, and my heart ſhall rejoice, even mine. How comfortably ſhould we ſhake hands with you, when you go abroad, were we perſwaded your ſouls were intereſted in Chriſt, and ſecured from periſhing, in the new covenant? What life would it put into our prayers for you, when you are abroad, to think that Jeſus Chriſt is interceeding for you in heaven, whilſt we are your remembrancers here on earth? How quiet would our hearts be when your are abroad in ſtorms; did we know you had a ſpecial intereſt in him whom winds and ſeas obey? To conclude, what joy would it be to your godly relations, to ſee you return new creatures? Doubtleſs more than if you came home laden with the riches of both *Indies*.

Come, Sirs! ſet the heavenly *Jeruſalem* upon the point of your *new Compaſs*; make all the ſail you can for it; and the Lord give you a proſperous gale, and a ſafe arrival in that land of reſt.

So prays

Your moſt *Affectionate Friend*
to ſerve you in Soul-Concernments.

JOHN FLAVEL.

IMPRIMATURE.

Ex. Æd. Lamb.
Dec. 14, 1663.

Geo. Strandling, *S T. P.*
Rev. in Christo Pat.
D. Gilb. de Archiepisc.
Cant. a Sac. Domest.

To every *Seaman* sailing Heaven-ward.

INGENIOUS SEAMAN.

THE art of navigation, by which Islands especially are enriched, and preserved in safety from forensical invasions; and the wonderful works of God in the great deep, and foreign nations are most delightfully and fully beheld, &c. is an art of exquisite excellency, ingenuity, rarity, and mirability: But the *Art of Spiritual Navigation* is the art of arts. It is a gallant thing to be able to carry a ship richly laden round the world: But it is much more gallant to carry a soul (that rich loading, a pearl of more worth than all the merchandise of the world) in a body (that is liable to leaks and bruises as any ship is) through the sea of this world (which is as unstable as water, and hath the same brinish taste and salt gust which the waters of the sea have) safe to heaven (the best haven) so as to avoid splitting upon any soul sinking rocks, or striking upon any soul drowning sands. The art of natural navigation is a very great mystery; but the art of spiritual navigation is by much a greater mystery. Human wisdom may teach us to carry a ship to the *Indies*; but the wisdom only that is from above can teach us to steer our course aright to the *haven* of *happiness*. This art is purely of *divine revelation*. The truth is, *divinity* (the doctrine of living to God) is nothing else but the *art of soul-navigation*, revealed from heaven. A meer man can carry a ship to any desired port in all the world, but no meer man can carry a soul to heaven. He must be a saint, he must be a divine (so all saints are) that can be a pilot to carry a soul to the *fair haven in Emanual's land*. The art of natural navigation is wonderfully improved since the coming of *Christ*, before which time (if there be truth in *history*) the use of the *loadstone* was never known in the world; and before the virtue of that was revealed unto the mariner, it is unspeakable with what uncertain wandrings seamen floated here and there, rather than sailed the right and direct way. Sure I am, the art of spiritual navigation is wonderfully improved since the coming of Christ: it oweth its clearest and fullest discovery to the coming of Christ. This art of arts is now perfectly revealed in the Scriptures of the Old and New Testament; but the rules thereof are dispersed up and down therein. The collecting and methodizing of the same, cannot but be a work very useful unto souls: Though when all is done, there is an absolute necessity of the teachings of the Spirit, and of the anointing that is from above, to make souls *artists* in sailing heavenward. The ingenious author of the Christian's Compass, or the Mariners Companion, makes three parts of this art (as the school men of divinity,) viz. *Speculative, Practical*, and *Affectionate*. The principal things necessary to be known by a spiritual seaman, in order to the steering rightly and safely to the *port* of happiness, he reduceth to four heads, answerable to the four general points of the Compass; making

God our *North*; *Christ* our *East*, *Holiness* our *South*, and *Death* our *West* points. Concerning God, we must know, 1. That he is, Heb. xi. 6. And that there is but one God, 1 Cor. viii. 5, 6. 2. That this God is that supreme good, in the enjoyment of whom all true happiness lies. Psa. iv. 6, 7. Mat. v. 8,——18, 20. 3. That (life eternal lying in God, and he being incomprehensible and inconceivable in essence, as being a Spirit) our best way to eye him is in his attributes, Exod. xxxiv. 5, 6, 7. And work, Rom. i. 20. And especially in his Son, 2 Cor. iv. 6, 4. That as God is a Spirit, so our chiefest, yea, only way of knowing, enjoying, serving, and walking with him, is in the spirit likewise, John iv. 24. Concerning Christ we must know, 1. That he is the true Sun which ariseth upon the world, by which all are enlightned, John i. ix. Mal. iii. 2. Luke i. 78, 79. 2. That God alone is in him, reconciling himself to the world, 2 Cor. v. 19. 1 Cor. i. 30. John xiv. 6. 3. That Jesus Christ is only made ours by the union and indwelling of himself in us through the spirit, 1. Cor. ii. 9, 10, and 6, 17. John xvi. 8, 9. 1 Cor. xii. 3, 13. 4. That the way of the spirit's uniting us to Christ, is by an act of power on his part, and by an act of faith on our parts, John iii. 16. last 5, 29. Eph. iii. 17. Concerning holiness, we must know, 1. That whoever is in Christ is a new creature, 2 Cor. v. 17. 1 Cor. vi. 11. 2. Holiness, is the souls highest lustre, Exod. xv. 11. When we come to perfection in holiness, then is our sun at the height in us. 3. Holiness, is Christ filling the soul; Christ our sun is at highest in our hearts, when they are most holy. 4. This holiness is that which is directly opposite to sin: sin eclipses holiness, and holiness scatters sin, Heb. vii. 26.

Phil. ii. 15. 2 Pet. iii. 11. Concerning death, we muſt know, 1. Death is certain : the ſun of our life will ſet in death ; when our days come about to this weſtern-point, it will be night, Heb. ix. 27. Pſa. xlxi. 7, 9. 2. If we die in our ſins out of Chriſt, we are undone forever, Job. viii. 24. Phil. i. 21. 3. It is our benighting to die, but it is not our annihilation, 1 Cor. xv. Rev. xx. 12. 4. After death comes judgment ; all that die ſhall ariſe to be judged, either for life or death the ſecond time, Heb. ix. 27. Mat. xxv. Heb. vi. 2. Theſe four heads, and the particulars under them are as neceſſary to be known in ſpiritual navigation, as the four points of the compaſs are in natural navigation. The things which we ought to do, in order to our arrival to our happineſs, our author makes as many as there are points in the compaſs. And for an help to memory, we may begin every particular with initial known letters on the points of the compaſs. 1. North. Never ſtir or ſteer any courſe, but by light from God, Pſa. cxix. 105. Iſa. viii. 10. 2. N. b. E. Never enter upon any deſign, but ſuch as tends towards Chriſt, Acts x. 43. 3. N. N. E. Note nothing envioufly, which thrives without God, Pſa. lxxiii. 12, 13. 4. N. E. b. N. Never enterprize not warrantable courſes, to procure any the moſt prized or conceited advantages, 1 Tim. vi. 9, 10. 5. N. N. E. Now entertain the ſacred commands of God, if hereafter thou expect the ſovereign conſolations of God, Pſa. cxix. 48, 6. N. E. b. E. Never eſteem *Egypt's* treaſures ſo much, as for them to forſake the people of God, Heb. 11. 26. 7. E. N. E. Err not, Eſpecially in foul affairs, James i. 16. 1 Tim. xix. 20. 2 Tim. ii. 18, 8. E. b. N. Eſchew nothing but ſin, 1 Pet. iii. 11. Job

i. 7. 8—31, 34. 9. E. Eſtabliſh thy heart with grace, Heb. xiii. 9. 10. E. b. S. Eye Sanctity in every action, 1 Pet. i. 15. Zech. xiv. 29. 11. E. S. E. Ever ſtrive earneſtly to live under, and to improve the means of grace. 12. S. E. b. E. Suffer every evil puniſhment of ſorrow, rather than leave the ways of Chriſt and Grace. 13. S. E. Sigh earneſtly for more enjoyments of Chriſt. 14. S. E. b. S. Seek ever more ſome evidences of Chriſt in you the hope of glory. 15. S. S. E. Still let eternity before you, in regard of enjoying Jeſus Chriſt, John xvii. 24. 16. S. b. E. Settle ever in your ſoul, as a principle which you will never depart from, that holineſs and true happineſs are in Chriſt and by Chriſt. 17. S. Set thyſelf always as before the Lord, Pſa. xvi. 8. Acts ii. 25. 18. S. b. W. See weakneſs haſtning thee to death, even when thou art at the higheſt pitch or point. 19. S. S. W. See ſin which is the ſting of death, as taken away by Chriſt, 1 Cor. xv. 55, 56. 20. S. W. b. S. Store up wiſely ſome proviſions every day for your dying day. 21. S. W. Set worldly things under your feet, before death come to look you in the face. 22. S. W. b. W. Still weigh and watch with loins girded and lamps trimmed, Luke xii. 35, 36. 37. 23. W. S. W. Weigh ſoul-works, and all in the balance of the ſanctuary. 24. W. b. S. Walk in ſweet communion with Chriſt here, and ſo thou maiſt die in peace, Luke ii. 29. 25. Weſt. Whatſoever thy condition be in this world, eye God as the difpoſer of it, and therein be contented, Phil. iv. 11. 26. W. b. N. Walk not according to the courſe of the moſt, but after the example of the beſt. 27. W. N. W. Weigh not what men ſpeak or think of thee, ſo God approve thee, 2 Chro. x. 18. Rom. ii. 28, 29.

28. N. W. b. W. Never wink at, but watch against small sins, nor neglect little duties, Eph. v. 15. 29. N. W. Never wish rashly for death, nor love life too inordinately, Job iii. 4. 30. N. W. b. N. Now work nimbly ere night come, John xii. 35, 36. Eccl. 9. 17. 31. N. N. W. Name nothing when thou pleadest with God for thy soul, but Christ and free grace, Dan. 9. 17. 32. N. b. W. Now welcome Christ, if at death thou wilt be welcomed by Christ. A tender, quick, enlivened and enlighted conscience, is the only point upon which we must erect these practical rules of our christian compass, Heb. xiii. 1. 2 Cor. i. 12. Our memory, that is the box in which this compass must be kept, in which these rules must be treasured, that we may be as ready and expert in them, as the mariner is in his sea compass. So much for the speculative and practical parts of the art of soul-spiritual-navigation. The affectionate part doth principally lie in the secret motions or movings of the soul towards God, in the affections which are raised and warmed, and especially appear active in meditation: meditation being as it were the limbeck or still in which the affections heat and melt, and as it were drop sweet spiritual waters. The affectionate author of the christian compass doth indeed, in the third and last part of his undertaking, hint at several meditations which the spiritual seaman is to be acquainted with, unto which thou hast an excellent supplement in this *new compays for seamen*. This collection is prefixt, that at once thou mayest view all the compasses (both the speculative, practical, and affectionate) by which thou must steer heavenward. What further shall be added by way of preface, is not to commend this new compass,

which indeed (2 Cor. iii. 1.) needs no *suftaticon epistolon*, *Letters of commendation*, or any panegyrick to usher it unto any honest heart : but to stir up all, especially seamen, to make conscience of using such choice helps for the promoting the sanctification and salvation of their souls, for the making of them as dexterous in the art of spiritual navigation, as any of them are in the art of natural navigation. Consider therefore,

1. What rich merchandize thy soul is. Christ assures us, one soul is more worth than all the world. The Lord Jesus doth as it were put the whole world in one scale, and one soul in the other, and the world is found too light, Mat. xvi. 26. Shouldst thou by skill in natural navigation carry safe all the treasures of the *Indies* into thine own port, yea, gain the whole world, and for want of skill in spiritual navigation lose thy soul, thou wouldst be the greatest loser in the world. So far wilt thou be from profiting by any of thy sea voyages. There is a plain *meiosis* in those words of Christ, *What is a man profited if he shall gain the whole world, and lose his own soul ? or what shall a man give in exchange for his soul ?* More is meant, than is spoken.

2. What a leaking vessel thy body is, in which this unspeakable inconceivable rich treasure, thy soul, is embarked ! O the many diseases and distempers in the humours and passions, that thy body is subject to ! It is above 2000 years ago, that there have been reckoned up 300 names of diseases ; and there be many under one name, and many nameless, which pose the physicians not only how to cure them, but how to call them. And for the affections and passions

Erasmi Chiliad, p. 299.

The smallest Pore is a Leak Wide enough to let in Death, and sink thy Vessel.

of the mind, the diftempers of them are no lefs deadly to fome, than the difeafes of the body. But befides thefe internal caufes, there are many external caufes of leaks in this veffel, as * poifonous malignities, wrathful hoftilities, and cafual mifhaps; very fmall matters may be of great moment to the finking of this veffel. The leaft Gnat in the Air may choak one, as it did *Adrian*, a Pope of *Rome*; a little hair in milk may ftrangle one, as it did a counfellor in *Rome*; a little ftone of a raifin may ftop ones breath as it did the poetical Poet *Anacreon*. Thus you fee what a leaking Veffel you fail in. Now the more leaky any fhip is, the more need there is of fkill to fteer wifely.

3. Confider what a dangerous Sea the World is, in which thy foul is to fail in the leaking fhip of thy body. As there are not more changes in the Sea, than are in the world being only conftant in inconftancy, *The fafhion of this world paffeth away*, 1 Cor. vii. 31. fo there are not more dangers in the feas for fhips, than there are in the world for fouls. In this world fouls meet with Rocks and fands, *Syrens* and Pirates. Worldly temptations, worldly luft, and worldly company caufe many to *drown themfelves in perdition*, 1 Tim. vi. 9. The very things of this world endanger our fouls. By worldly objects we foon grow worldly. It is hard to touch pitch, and not be defiled. The lufts of this world ftain our glory, and the men of this world pollute all they converfe with. A man that keeps company with the men of this world, is like him that walketh in the Sun, tanned infenfibly. Thus,

C

---

* In Nubia, quæ eft Æthiopia, venenum eft cujus grani unius decima pars hominem, vel unum granum decem homines, *Dan. Senert* Hypom. Phyf. Cap. 2. p. 47.

you have hinted the dangerousness of the Sea, wherein you are to sail. Now, the more dangerous the Sea is, the more requisite it is the sailor be an artist.

4. Consider, what if through want of skill in the heavenly Art of Spiritual Navigation, thou shouldst not steer thy Course aright! I will instance only in two consequents thereof. 1 Thou shalt arrive at the heaven of happiness. 2 Thou shalt be drowned in the Ocean of God's wrath. As true as the word of God is true; as sure as the Heavens are over thy head, and the Earth under thy feet; as sure as thou yet livest and breathest in this Air; so true and certain it is, thou shalt never enter into heaven, but sink into the depth of the bottomless pit. Am I not herein a messenger of the saddest tidings that ever yet thy Ears did hear? Possibly now thou makest a light matter of these things, because thou dost not know what it is to miss of heaven, and what it is for ever to lie under the wrath of God: but hereafter thou wilt know fully, what it is to have thy soul lost eternally, so lost, as that God's mercies, and all the good there is in Christ, shall never save it; and as God hath set and ordered things, can never save it. Hereafter thou wilt be perfectly sensible of the good that thou mightest have had, and of the evil that shall be upon thee (this is God's preculiar prerogative, to make a Creature as sensible of misery as he pleaseth,) then thou wilt have other thoughts of these things than now thou hast. Then the thoughts of thy mind shall be busied about thy lost Condition, both as to the pain of loss, and pain of sense; so that thou shalt not be able to take any ease any moment: then, that thy

Ignis Gehennæ lucebit miseris, ut videant unde doleant. Insid. de sum. bon. l. 1.

torments may be increased, thy knowledge, the truth of thy apprehensions, yea, the strength of them, shall be increased; thou shalt have true and deep apprehensions of the greatness of that good that thou shalt miss of, and of that evil which thou shalt procure unto thy self; and then thou shalt not be able to choose, but to apply all thy loss, all thy misery to thy self, which will force thee to roar out, O my loss! O my misery! O my unconceivable unrecoverable loss and misery! Yea, for the increasing of thy torments, thy affections and memory shall be enlarged: O that, to prevent that loss and memory shall be enlarged: O that, to prevent that loss and misery, these things may now be known and laid to heart! O that blind Understanding, a stupid judgment, a bribed conscience, a hard heart, a bad memory, may no longer make heaven and hell to seem but trifles to thee! Thou wilt then easily be persuaded to make it thy main business here, to become an artist in *spiritual navigation*. But to shut up this preface, I shall briefly acquaint *Seamen*, why they should of all others, be men of singular piety and heavenliness, and therefore more than ordinarily study the heavenly art of *spiritual Navigation*. O that *Seamen* would therefore consider,

1. How nigh they border upon the confines of death and eternity every moment. There is but a step, but an inch or two between them and their graves continually. The next gust may over-set them; the next wave may swallow them up. In one place lies lurking dangerous rocks, in another perilous sands, and every where stormy winds, ready to destroy them. Well may the *Seamen* cry out, *Ego crastinum non habui*; I have not had a morrow in my hands these many years. Should

<small>Terror ubique tremor, timor undiq, & undiq; tenari. Ovi.</small>

not they then be extraordinary serious and heavenly continually? Certainly (as the reverend Author of this *New Compass* well observes) nothing more composeth the heart to such a frame than the lively apprehensions of eternity do: and none have greater external advantages for that, than *Seamen* have.

2. Consider *(Seamen)* what extraordinary help you have by the book of the creature; the whole creation is God's voice, it is God's excellent handwriting, or the Sacred Scriptures of the Most High to teach us much of God, and what reasons we have to bewail our rebellion against God, and to make conscience of obeying God only, naturally and continually. The heavens, the earth, the waters are the three great leaves of this Book of God, and all the creatures are so many lines in those leaves. All that learn not to fear and serve God by the help of this book will be left inexcusable, *Rom.* i. 20. How inexcusable then will ignorant and ungodly *Seamen* be? *Seamen* should in this respect, be the best Scholars in the Lord's School, seeing they do more, than others, see the works of the Lord, and his wonders in the great deep, Pfal. cvii. 24.

Mundi creatio est Scriptura Dei, Clemens. Universus mundus est deus explicatus.

3. Consider how often, you are nearer heaven than any people in the world. *They mount up to heaven*, Pfal. cvii. 26. It has been said of an ungodly minister, who contradicted his preaching in his life and conversation, That it was pity he should ever come out of the pulpit, because he was there as near heaven as ever he would be. Shall it be said of you, upon the same account, That 'tis pity you should come down from the high towering waves of the sea? Should not *Seamen*, that in stormy weather have their feet (as it were) upon the

battlements of heaven, look down upon all earthly happiness in this world but as base, waterish, and worthless? The great cities of *Campania* seem but small cottages to them that stand on the *Alpes*. Should not *Seamen*, that so often mount up to heaven, make it their main business here, once at last to get into heaven? What *(seamen)* shall you only go to heaven against your wills? When *seamen* mount up to heaven in a storm, the *Psalmist* tells us, that *their souls are melted because of trouble.* O that you were continually as unwilling to go to hell, as you are in a storm to go to heaven!

4. -And lastly, Consider what engagements ly upon you to be singularly holy, from your singular deliverances & salvations. They that go down to the sea in ships, are sometimes in the valley of the shadow of death, by reason of the springing of perilous leaks; and yet miraculously delivered, either by some wonderful stopping of the leak, or by God's sending some ships within their sight, when they have been far out of sight of any land; or by his bringing their near perishing ships safe to shore Sometimes they have been in very great danger of being taken by pirates, yet wonderfully preserved, either by God's calming of the winds in that part of the sea where the Pirates have sailed, or by giving the poor pursued ship a strong gale of wind to run away from their pursuers; or by sinking the Pirates, &c. Sometimes their ships have been cast away, & yet they themselves wonderfully got safe to shore upon planks, yards, masts, &c. I might be endless in enumerating their deliverances from drowning, from burning, from slavery, &c. Sure *(seamen)* your extraordinary salvations lie more than ordinary engagements upon you, to praise, love, fear, obey and trust in your saviour and deliverer. I have read, that

the enthralled *Greeks* were fo affected with their liberty, procured by *Flaminius* the *Roman* general, that their fhrill acclamations of *Soter, Soter, A Sáviour, a Saviour,* made the very birds fall down from the heavens aftonifhed. O how fhould *feamen* be affected with their *fea-deliverances!* Many that have been delivered from *Turkifh flavery,* have vowed to be fervants to their *Redeemers* all the days of their lives. Ah, Sirs, will you not be more than ordinarily God's fervants all the days of your lives. Seeing you have been fo oft, fo wonderfully redeemed from death itfelf by him? Verily, do what you can, you will die in God's debt. *As for me, God forbid, that I fhould fin againft the Lord, in ceafing to pray for you,* 1 Sam. xii. 23, 24. That by the perufal of this fhort and fweet treatife, wherein the judicious and ingenious author hath well mixed *utile dulci,* profit and pleafure, you may learn the good and right way, even to fear the Lord, and ferve him in truth with all your hearts, confidering how great things he hath done for you: This is the hearty prayer of

Your cordial Friend, earneftly defirous of a profperous Voyage for your precious and immortal Souls. T. M.

THE AUTHOR TO THE READER.

"WHEN dewy-cheeck'd *Aurora* doth display
"Her curtains, to let in the new-born day,
"Her heavenly face looks red, as if it were
"Dy'd with a modest blush, 'twixt shame and fear.
"*Sol* makes her blush, suspecting that he will
"Scorch some too much, and others leave to chill,
"With such a blush, my little new-born book
"Goes out of hand, suspecting some may look
"Upon it with contempt, while others raise
"So mean a piece too high, by flattering praise.
"Its beauty cannot make its father dote;
"'Tis a poor babe, clad in a sea-green coat.
"Its gone from me too young, and now is run
"To sea, among the tribe of *Zebulon*.
"Go, little book, thou many friends wilt find
"Among that tribe, who will be very kind;
"And many of them care of thee will take,
"Both for thy own, and for thy father's sake.
"Heaven save it from the dangerous storms and gusts
"That will be rais'd against it by men's lusts.
"Guilt makes men angry, anger is a storm;
"But sacred truth's thy shelter, fear no harm.
"On times, on persons, no reflections found;
"Though with reflection few books more abound.
"Go, little book, I have much more to say,
"But sea-men call for thee, thou must away.
"Yet ere you have it, grant me one request;
"Pray do not keep it prisoner in your chest."

A NEW COMPASS FOR SEAMEN,

OR

NAVIGATION

SPIRITUALIZED.

CHAP. I.

*The launching of a ship plainly sets forth
Our double state, by first and second birth.*

OBSERVATION.

NO sooner is a ship built, launched, rigged, victualled, and manned, but she is presently sent out into the boisterous ocean, where she is never at rest, but continually fluctuating, tossing and labouring, until she be either overwhelmed and wrecked, in the sea, or through age, knocks and bruises, grows leaky and unserviceable; and so is hauled up, and ript abroad.

APPLICATION.

No sooner come we into the world as men, or as christians, by a natural, or supernatural birth; but thus we are tost upon a sea of troubles, Job. v. 7. *Yet man is born to trouble, as sparks flie upwards.* The spark no sooner comes out of the fire, but it flies up naturally; it needs not any external force, help, or guidance, but ascends from a principle in itself: So naturally, so easily, doth trouble rise out of sin. There is *radically* all the misery, anguish, and trouble in the world, in our corrupt natures. As the spark lies close hid in the coals, so doth misery in sin: Every sin draws a rod after it. And these sorrows and troubles fall not only on the body, in those breaches, flaws, deformities, pains, aches, diseases to which it is subject, which are but the groans of dying nature, and its crumbling, by degrees, into dust again; but on all our imployments and callings also, Gen. iii. 17, 18, 19. These are full of pain, trouble, and disappointment. Hag. i. 6. We earn wages, and put it into a bag with holes, and disquiet ourselves in vain; all our relations are full of trouble. The apostle speaking to those that marry, saith, 1 Cor. vii. 28. *Such shall have trouble in the flesh.* Upon which words one glasseth thus: Flesh and trouble are married together, whether we marry or no: But they that are married, marry with, and match into new troubles: All relations have their burdens, as well as their comforts. It were endless to enumerate the sorrows of this kind and yet the troubles of the body, are but the body of troubles: The spirit of the curse falls upon the

See Mr. Bursleii's Care Cloth.

spiritual and noblest part of man. The soul and body, like to *Ezekial's* roll, are written full with sorrows, both within and without. So that we make the same report of our lives, when we come to die, that old *Jacob* made before *Pharaoh*, Gen. xlvii. 9. *Few and evil have the days of the years of our lives been. For what hath man of all his labour, and of the vexation of his heart, wherein he hath laboured under the sun? For all his days are sorrows and his travel grief, yea, his heart taketh no rest in the night: This is also vanity*, Eccles. ii. 22, 23.

Neither doth our new birth free us from troubles, though then they be sanctified, sweetned, and turned into blessings to us. We put not off the humane, when we put on the divine nature; nor are we then freed from the sense, though we be delivered from the sting and curse of them. Grace doth not presently pluck out all those arrows that sin hath shot into the sides of nature, 2 Cor. vii. 5. *When we were come into Macedonia, our flesh had no rest, but we were troubled on every side: without were fightings and within were fears*, Rev. vii. 14. *These are they that came out of great tribulation.* The first cry of the Newborn christian (says one) gives hell an alarm, and awakens the rage, both of devils and men against him. Hence *Paul* and *Barnabas* acquainted those new converts, Acts xiv. 22. "That through much tribulation, they must enter into the kingdom of God:" And we find the state of the church, in this world, set out. (Isa. liv. 11. by the similitude of a distressed ship at sea: *O thou afflicted (and tossed) with tempests, and not comforted.* (Tossed) as *Jonas'* ship was; for the same word is there used, *Jonah* i. 11, 13. As a vessel at sea, stormed, and violently driven without *rudder, mast, sail, or tacklings.* Nor are we to expect freedom from those troubles, until harboured in heaven, see 2 Thess. i. vii. O what large catalogues of experiences do the saints carry to heaven with them, of their various exercises, dangers, trials, and marvellous preservations and deliverances out of all! And yet all these troubles without, are nothing to those within them; from temptations, corruption, desertions, by passion and compassion: Besides their own, there comes daily upon them the troubles of others; many rivulets fall into this channel and brim, yea often overflow the banks, Psal. xxxiv. 19. *Many are the afflictions of the righteous.*

REFLECTION.

Hence should the graceless heart thus reflect upon itself. O my soul! into what a sea of troubles art thou launched forth! And what a sad case thou art in! Full of trouble, and full of sin, and these do mutually produce each other. And that which is the most dreadful consideration of all, is, That I cannot see the end of them. As for the saints, they suffer in the world as well as I; but it is but for a while, 1 Pet. v. 10. And then they shall suffer no more, 2 Thess. i. 7. But *all tears shall be wiped away from their eyes*, Rev. vii. 17. But thy troubles look with a long visage: Ah! they are but the beginning of sorrows, but a parboiling before I be roasted in the flames of God's eternal wrath. If I continue as I am, I shall but deceive myself, if I conclude I shall be happy in the other world, because I have met with so much sorrow in this: For I read, Jude vii. that the inhabitants of *Sodom* and *Gomorrah*, though consumed to ashes, with all their estates and relations, (a sorer temporal judgment than ever yet befel me) do notwithstanding that, continue still in "everlasting chains, under darkness in which they are reserved unto the judgment of the great day." The troubles of the saints are sanctified to them, but mine are fruits of the curse. They have spiritual consolations to ballance them, which flow into their souls in the same height and degree as troubles do upon their bodies, 2 Cor. i. 5. But I am a stranger to their comforts, and *intermeddle not with their joys*, Prov. xiv. 10. If their hearts be surcharged with trouble, they have a God to go to; and when they have opened their cause before him, they are eased, return with comfort, and their *countenance is no more sad*, 1 Sam. i. 18. When their belly is as bottles full of new wine, they can give it vent by pouring out of their souls into their father's bosom: But I have no interest in, nor acquaintance with this God; nor can I pray unto him in the spirit. My griefs are shut up like fire in my bosom, which preys upon my spirit. This is my sorrow, and I alone must bear it. O my soul, look round about thee! What a miserable case art thou in? Rest no longer satisfied in it, but look out for a Christ also. What though I be a vile unworthy wretch? yet he promiseth to *love freely*, Hos. xiv. 4. And invites such as are heavy laden to him, Mat. xi. 28.

Hence also should the gracious soul reflect sweetly upon itself after this manner: And is the world so full of trouble? O my soul, what cause hast thou to stand admiring at the indulgence and goodness of God to thee! Thou hast hitherto had a smooth passage comparatively to what others have had. How hath divine wisdom ordered my condition, and cast my lot? Have I been chastised with whips? Others with scorpoins: Have I had no peace without: Some have neither had peace without nor within, but terrors round about: Or have I felt trouble in my flesh and spirit at once? Yet have they not been extream, either for time or measure. And hath the world been a *Sodom*, an *Egypt* to thee? Why then doft thou thus linger in it, and hanker after it? Why do I not long to be gone, and figh more heartily for deliverance? Why are the thoughts of my Lord's coming no fweeter to me, and the day of my full deliverance no more panted for? And why am I no more careful to maintain peace within, fince there is fo much trouble without? Is not this it that puts weight into all outward troubles, and makes them finking, that they fall upon me when my fpirit is dark or wounded?

THE POEM.

" My foul art thou befieged

" With troubles round about?

" If thou be wife, take this advice,

" To keep thefe troubles out.

" Wife men will *keep* their confcience as their eyes;

" For in their *confcience* their beft treafure lies.

" See you be *tender* of your inward peace:

" That fhipwreck, *then* your mirth and joy muft ceafe.

" If God from *you* your outward comforts rend,

" You'll find what *need* you have of fuch a friend.

" If this be *not* by fin deftroyed and loft,

" You need not *fear*, your peace will quit your coft.

" If you know *how* to fweeten any grief,

" Though ne'er fo great, or to procure relief,

" Againft th' *afflictions*, which like deadly darts

" Moft fatal *are* to men of carnal hearts,

"Reject not *that* which conscience bids you chuse,
"And chuse not *you*, what conscience faith, refuse,
"If sin you *must*, or misery under lie,
"Resolve to *bear*, and chuse the misery."

CHAP. II.

In the vast Ocean spiritual eyes descry,
God's boundless mercy, and eternity.

OBSERVATION.

THE ocean is of vast extent and depth, though supposedly measurable, yet not to be sounded by man. It compasseth about the whole earth, which in the account of geographers, is twenty one thousand and six hundred miles in compass; yet the ocean invirons it on every side, Psal. civ. 25. And Job xi. 9. Suitable to which is that of the poet.

Tum freta diffudit, rapidisque tumescere ventis
Jussit & ambitæ circumdare littora terrae. Ovid.

He spread the seas, which then he did command,
To swell with winds, and compass round the land.

And for its depth, who can discover it? The sea in scripture is called, *The deep*, Job xxxviii. 30. The *Great deep*, Gen. vii. 11. The gathering together of the *waters* into one place, Gen. i. 9. If the vastest mountain were cast into it, it would appear on more than the head of a pin in a ton of water.

APPLICATION.

This in a lively manner shadows forth the infinite and incomprehensible mercy of our God; whose mercy is said to be over all his works, Psal. clv. 9. In how many sweet notions is the mercy of God represented to us in the scripture. He is said to be *plenteous*, Psal. cxxx. 7. *Abundant*, 1 Pet. i. 3. *Rich*, Eph. ii. 4. *In mercy*; then, that his mercies are *unsearchable*, Eph. iii. 8. *High as the heaven above the earth*, Psal. xxxvi. 5. Which are so high and vast, that the whole earth is but a small point to them: yea, they are not only compared to the heavens, but to come home to the *metaphor*, to the depths of the sea, Mic. vii. 19. Which can swallow up mountains as well as mole-hills; and in this sea God had drowned sins of a dreadful height and aggravation, even *scarlet, crimson* (*i. e.*) deep dyed with many intensive aggravations, Isa. i. 18. In this sea was the sin of *Manasseh* drowned; and of what magnitude that was, may be seen, 2 Chron. xxxiii. 3. Yea, in this ocean of mercy, did the Lord drown and cover the sins of *Paul*, though a blasphemer, a persecutor, injurious, 1 Tim. i. 13. "None, saith *Augustine*, more fierce than *Paul* among the persecutors; and therefore none greater among sinners:" To which himself willingly subscribes, 1 Tim. i. 15. *Yet pardoned.* How hath mercy rode in triumph, and been glorified upon the vilest of men! How hath it stopt the slanderous mouth of men and devils! it hath yearned upon *fornicators, idolators, adulterers, thieves, covetous, drunkards, revilers, extortioners*, to such hath the sceptre of mercy been stretched forth, upon their unfeigned repentance and submission, 1 Cor. vi. 9.

What doth the spirit of God aim at, in such a large accumulation of names of mercy? But to convince poor sinners of the abundant fulness and riches of it, if they will but submit to the terms on which it is tendered to them.

In the vastness of the ocean, we have also a lively emblem of eternity. Who can comprehend or measure the ocean, but God? And who can comprehend eternity, but he that is said *to inhabit it?* Isa. lvii. 15. Though shallow rivers may be drained and dried up, yet the ocean cannot. And though these transitory days, months, and years will at last expire and determine; yet eternity shall not. O! it is a long world! and amazing matter! What is eternity, but a constant permnanancy of persons and things, in one and the same state and condition for ever; putting them beyond all possibility of change? The heathens were wont to shadow it by a circle, or a snake twisted round. It will be to all of us, either a perpetual day or night, which will not be measured by watches, hours, minutes. And as it cannot be measured, so neither can it ever be diminished. When thousands of years are gone, there is not a minute less to come. *Gerhard* and *Drexellius* do both illustrate it by this known similitude: Suppose a bird were to come once in a thousand years, to some vast mountain of sand, and carry away in her bill one sand in a thousand years; O what a vast time would it be, before that immortal bird, after that rate, had recovered the mountain! yet in time this might be done. For there would be still some diminution; but in eternity there can be none. There be three things in time which are not competent to eternity: In time there is a *succession*, one generation, year, and day paſſeth, and another comes ; but eternity is a fixed (*now*.) In time there is a *diminution* and waſting ; the more is paſt, the leſs to come : But it is not ſo in eternity. In time there is an *alteration* of condition and ſtates : A man may be poor to day, and rich tomorrow ; ſickly and diſeaſed this week, and well the next; now in contempt, and anon in honour : But no change paſſes upon us in eternity. As the tree falls at death and judgment, ſo it lies forever. If in heaven, there thou art a pillar, and ſhalt go forth no more, Rev. iii. 12. If in hell, no redemption thence, but the ſmoak of their torments aſcendeth for ever and ever, Rev. xix. 3.

REFLECTION.

And is the mercy of God, like the great deeps, an ocean, that none can fathom? What unſpeakable comfort is this to me ? may the pardoned ſoul ſay. Did *Iſrael* ſing a ſong, when the Lord had overwhelmed their corporal enemies in the ſeas ? And ſhall not I break forth into his praiſes, who hath drowned all my ſins in the depths of mercy ? O my ſoul, bleſs thou the Lord, and let his high praiſes ever be in thy mouth. Mayſt not thou ſay, that he hath gone to as high an extent and degree of mercy, in pardoning thee, as ever he did in any? Oh my God, who is like unto thee! that pardoneſt iniquity, tranſgreſſion and ſin. What mercy, but the mercy of a God, could cover ſuch abominations as mine !

But O ! what terrible reflections will conſcience make from hence, upon all the deſpiſers of mercy, when the ſinners eyes come to be opened too late for mercy, to do them good ! We have heard indeed, that the King of heaven was a merciful King, but we would make no addrefs to him, whilſt that Scepter was ſtretched out. We heard of balm in *Gilead*, and a phyſician there, that was able and willing to cure all our wounds, but would not commit ourſelves to him. We read that the arms of Chriſt were open to embrace and receive us, but we would not. O unparallel'd folly! O ſoul-deſtroying madneſs? Now the womb of mercy is ſhut up, and ſhall bring forth no more mercies to me for ever. Now the gates of grace are ſhut, and no cries can open them.

Mercy acted its part, and is gone off the ſtage; and now juſtice enters the ſcene and will be glorified for ever upon me. How often did I hear the bowels of compaſſion ſounding in the goſpel for me? But my hard and impenitent heart could not relent; and now, if it could, it is too late. I am now paſt out of the ocean of mercy, into the ocean of eternity, where I am fixed in the midſt of endleſs miſery, and ſhall never hear the voice of mercy more.

O dreadful eternity! Oh ſoul-confounding word! An ocean indeed, to which this ocean is but as a drop; for in thee no ſoul ſhall ſee either bank or bottom. If I lie but one night under ſtrong pains of body, how tedious doth that night ſeem! And how do I tell the clock, and wiſh for day! In the world I might have had life, and would not; And now, how fain would I have death, but cannot? How quick were my ſins in execution? And how long is their puniſhment in duration? O, how ſhall I dwell with everlaſting burnings? Oh that God would but vouchſafe one treaty more with me! But alas, all tenders and treaties are now at an end with me. On earth peace, Luke ii. 14. But none in hell. O my ſoul conſider theſe things: come, let us debate this matter seriously, before we launch out into this ocean.

THE POEM.

"Who from some high-rais'd tower views the ground,
"His heart doth tremble, and his head doth round:
"Even so my soul, whilst it doth view and think
"On this eternity, upon whose brink
"It borders, stands amazed, and doth cry,
"O boundless! bottomless eternity!
"The scourge of hell, whose very lash doth rend
"The damned souls in twain: What! never end?
"The more thereon they ponder, think and pore,
"The more, poor wretches, still they howl and roar.
"Ah! through more years in torments we should lie,
"Than sands are on the shore, or in the skie
"Are twinkling stars: yet this gives some relief,
"The hope of ending. Ah! but here's the grief!
"A thousand years in torments past and gone,
"Ten thousand more afresh are coming on;
"And when these thousands all their course have run,
"The end's no more than when at first begun.
"Come then, my soul, let us discourse together
"This weighty point, and tell me plainly whether
"You for these short-liv'd points, that come and go,
"Will plunge yourself and me in endless woe.
"Resolve the question quickly, do not dream
"More time away. Lo, in an hasty stream
"We swiftly pass, and shortly we shall be
"Ingulphed both in this eternity.

CHAP. III.

Within these smooth-faced seas strange creatures crawl,
But in man's heart, far greater than them all.

OBSERVATION.

IT was an unadvised saying of *Plato*, *Mare nil memorabile producit* : The sea produceth nothing memorable. But surely there is much of the wisdom, power, and goodness of God manifested in those inhabitants of the watery region : Notwithstanding the seas azure and smiling face, strange creatures are bred in its womb. "O Lord, (saith David) how manifold are thy works ? In wisdom hast thou made them all ; the earth is full of thy riches. So is this great and wide sea, wherein are things creeping innumerable, both small and great beasts, Psa. civ. 24, 25. And we read, Lam. iv. 3. of *sea-monsters, which draw out their breasts to their young.* *Pliny* and *Purchas* tell incredible stories about them. About the topick of *Capricorn*, our seamen meet with flying fishes, that have wings like a *rere-mouse*, but of a silver colour ; they fly in flocks like *stares*. There are creatures of very strange forms and properties ; some resembling a cow, called by the *Spaniards*, *Manates*, by some supposed to be the sea-monster spoken of by *Jeremy*. In the rivers of *Guiana*, *Purchas* saith, there are fishes that have four eyes, bearing two above and two beneath the water when they swim : some resembling a toad, and very poisonous. How strange both in shape and property is the *sword fish* and *thrasher*, that fights with the *whale*? Even our own seas produce creatures of strange shapes, but the commonness takes off the wonder.

APPLICATION.

Thus doth the heart of man naturally swarm and abound with strange and monstruous lusts and abominations, Rom. i. 29, 30, 31. "Being filled with all unrighteous, fornication, wickedness, covetousness, maliciousness, full of envy, murder, debate, deceit, malignity, whisperers, back-biters, haters of God, despiteful, proud, boasters, inventors of evil things, disobedient to parents, without understanding, covenant-breakers, without natural affection, implacable, unmerciful." O what a swarm is here! and yet there are multitudes more, in the depth of the heart! and it is no wonder, considering that with this nature, we received the spawn of the blackest and vilest abominations. This original lust is productive to them all, James i. 14, 15. Which lust, though it be in every man *numerically* different from that of others, yet it is one and the same *specifically*, for sort and kind, in all the children of *Adam*: even as the reasonable soul, though every man hath his own soul, *viz.* a soul individually distinct from another man's, yet is it the same for kind in all men. So that whatever abominations are in the hearts and lives of the vilest *Sodomites*, and most profligate wretches under heaven, there is the same matter in thy heart out of which they were shaped and formed. In the depths of the heart they are conceived, and thence they crawl out of the eyes, hands, lips, and all the members, Mat. xv. 18, 19. " Those things (saith Christ) which proceed out of the mouth, come forth from the heart, and defile a man. For out of the heart proceed evil thoughts, murders, adulteries, fornications, thefts, false witness, blasphemies:" Even such monsters, as would make a gracious heart tremble to behold. "What are my lusts, (saith one) but so many toads spitting of venom, and spawning of poison; croaking in my judgment, creeping in my will, and crawling into my affections?" The Apostle in 1 Cor. v. 1. Tells us of a sin, *Not to be named*; so monstrous that nature itself startles at it: even such monsters are generated in the depths of the heart. Whence come evils? Was a question that much puzzled the philosophers of old. Now here you may see whence they come, and where they are begotten.

Fuller's Meditations, p. 11.

REFLECTION.

And are there such strange abominations in the heart of man? then how is he degenerated from his primitive perfection and glory! his streams were once as clear as a crystal, and the fountain of them pure, there was no unclean creature moving in them. What a stately fabrick was the soul at first! and what holy inhabitants possessed the several rooms thereof? But now (as God speaks of *Idumea*) Isa. xxxiv. 11. "The line of confusion is stretched out upon it, and the stones of emptiness. The cormorant and bittern possess it; the owl and the raven dwell in it." Yea wild beasts of the desart lie there; it is full of doleful creatures, the satyres dance in it, and dragons cry in those sometimes pleasant places." O sad change! how sadly may we look back towards our first state! and take up the words of *Job*, "O that I were as in months past, as in the days of my youth; when the Almighty, was yet with me, when I put on righteousness, and it cloathed me; when my glory was fresh in me," Job xxix. 2, 4, 5.

Again, think O my soul what a miserable condition the unregenerate abide in! thus swarmed and over-run with hellish lusts, under the dominion and vassalage of divers lusts, Tit. iii. 3. What a tumultuous sea is such a soul! How do these lusts rage within them! how do they contest and scuffle for the throne! and usually take it by turns: For as all diseases are contrary to health, yet some contrary to each other, so are lusts. Hence poor creatures are hurried on to different kinds of servitude, according to the nature of that imperious lust that is in the throne; and like the lunatick, Mat. 17. Are sometimes cast into the *water*; and sometimes into the *fire*. Well might the prophet say, "The wicked is like a troubled sea that cannot rest," Isa. lvii. 20. They have no peace now in the service of sin, and less they shall have hereafter, when they receive the wages of sin. "There is no peace to the wicked, saith my God." They indeed cry, *Peace, peace*; but my God doth not say so. The last issue and result of this is eternal death; no sooner is it delivered of its deceitful pleasures, but presently it falls in travail again, and brings forth death, James i. 15.

Once more: and is the heart such a sea, abounding with monstrous abominations? then stand astonished, O my soul, at that free grace which hath delivered thee from so sad a condition! O fall down, and kiss the feet of mercy that moved so freely and seasonably to thy rescue! let my heart be enlarged abundantly here. Lord, what am I, that I should be taken, and others left? Reflect, O my soul, upon the conceptions and births of lusts, in the days of vanity, which thou now blusheft to own. O what black imaginations, hellish desires, vile affections, are lodged there! Who made me to differ? or, how came I to be thus wonderfully separated? surely, it is by thy free grace, and nothing else, that I am what I am: and by that grace I have escaped (to mine own astonishment) the corruption that is in the world through lust. O that ever the holy God should set his eyes on such an one: or cast a look of love towards me, in whom were regions of unclean lusts and abominations!

THE POEM.

" My soul's the sea wherein from day to day,
" Sins like Leviathans do sport and play.
" Great master-lusts, with all the lesser fry,
" Therein increase, and strangely multiply.
" Yet strange it is not, sin so fast should breed,
" Since with this nature I received the seed
" And spawn of every species, which was shed
" Into its caverns first, then nourished
" By its own native warmth: which like the sun,
" Hath quickened them, and now abroad they come,
" And like the frogs of Egypt creep and crawl
" Into the closest rooms within my soul.
" My fancy swims, for there they frisk and play,
" In dreams by night, and foolish toys by day.
" My judgment's clouded by them, and my will

"Perverted every corner they do fill.
"As locusts seize on all that's fresh and green,
"Uncloath the beauteous spring, and make it seem
"Like drooping Autumn; so my soul, that first
"As Eden seem'd, now's like a ground that's curst.
"Lord purge my streams, and kill these lusts that lie
"Within them; if thou do not, I must die.

CHAP. IV.

*Seas purge themselves, and cast their filth ashore;
But graceless souls retain, and suck in more.*

OBSERVATION.

SEAS are in a continual motion and agitation; they have their flux and reflux, by which they are kept from putrefaction: like a fountain it cleanses itself, Isa. 57. 20. "It cannot rest but cast up mire and dirt;" whereas lakes and ponds, whose waters are standing, and dead, corrupt and stink. And it is observed by sea-men, that in the southern parts of the world, where the sea is more calm and settled, it is more corrupt and unfit for use; so is the sea of *Sodom* called *The dead Sea.*

APPLICATION.

Thus do regenerate souls purify themselves, and work out corruption that defiles them, they cannot suffer it to settle there, 1 John iii. 3. "He purifieth himself, even as he is pure. Keeping himself, that the wicked one toucheth him not," 1 John

v. 18. Scil. *Tacto qualitativo*, with a qualitative touch, as the load-stone toucheth iron, leaving an impression of its nature behind it. They are doves delighting in cleanness, Isa. xxxiii. 15. " He despiseth the gain of oppression, he shaketh his hands from holding of bribes, stoppeth his ears from hearing blood, and shutteth his eyes from seeing evil." See how all senses and members are guarded against sin : but it is quite contrary with the wicked ; there is no principle of holiness in them, to oppose or expel corruption. It lies in their hearts as mud in a lake or well, which settles and corrupts more and more. Hence Ezek. xlvii. 11. Their hearts are compared to miry or marish places, which cannot be healed, but are given to salt: The meaning is, that the purest streams of the gospel, which cleanse others, make them worse than before, as abundance of rain will a miry place. The reason is, because it meets with an obstacle in their souls ; so that it cannot run through them and be glorified, as it doth in gracious souls. All the means and endeavours used to cleanse them, are in vain; all the grace of God they receive in vain : " They hold fast deceit, they refuse to let it go," Jer. viii. 5. Sin is not in them as floating weeds upon the sea, which it strives to expel and purge out, but as *spots* in the *leopards* skin, Jer. xiii. 21. Or letters fashioned and engraven in the very substance of marble or brass, with a pen of iron, and point of a diamond, Jer. xvii. 1. Or as ivy in an old wall, that hath got rooting into its very intrails. " Wickedness is sweet in their mouths, they roul it under their tongues," Job xx. 12. No threats nor promises can divorce them from it.

REFLECTION.

Lord! this is the very frame of my heart, may the graceless soul say: my corruptions quietly settle in me, my heart labours not against it: I am a stranger to that conflict which is daily maintained in all the faculties of the regenerate soul. Glorified souls have no such conflict, because grace in them stands alone, and is perfectly triumphant over all its opposites; and graceless souls can have no such conflict, because in them corruption stands alone, and hath no other principle to make opposition to it. And this is my case, O Lord: I am full of vain hopes indeed, but had I a living and well-grounded hope to dwell forever with so holy a God, I could not but be daily purifying myself. But O! what will the end of this be? I have cause to tremble at that last and dreadfullest curse in the book of God, Rev. xxii. 11. "Let him that is filthy be filthy still." Is it not as much as if God should say, Let them alone, I will spend no more rods upon them, no more means shall be used about them; but I will reckon with them for all together in another world; O my soul! what a dismal reckoning will that be! ponder with thyself in the mean while, those terrible and awakening texts, that if possible, this fatal issue may be prevented. See Isa. i. 5. Hos. iv. 14. Jer. vi. 29, 30. Heb. vi. 8.

THE POEM.

"My heart's no fountain, but a standing lake
"Of putrid waters; if therein I rake,
"By serious search, O! what a noisome smell,
"Like exhalations rising out of hell;
"The stinking waters pump'd up from the hole,
"Are as perfumes to sea-men: but my soul
"Upon the same account that they are glad,
"(Its long continuance there) is therefore sad.
"The scripture saith, *No soul God's face shall see*
"Till from such filthy lusts it cleansed be.
"Yet though unclean, it may that way be rid,
"As *Hercules* the *Augean* stable did.
"Lord turn into my soul that cleansing blood,
"Which from my Saviour's side flow'd as a flood.
"Flow, sacred fountain, brim my banks; and flow
"Till you have made my soul as white as snow.

CHAP. V.

Seamen fore-see a danger, and prepare:
Yet few of greater dangers are aware.

OBSERVATION.

HOW watchful and quick-sighted are seamen, to prevent dangers? If the wind die away, and then fresh up southerly; or if they see the sky hazy, they provide for a storm: if by the prospective glass they ken a *pirate* at the greatest distance, they clear the gun-room, prepare for fight, and bear up, if able to deal with him; if not, they keep close by the wind, make all the sail they can, and bear away. If they suppose themselves by their reckoning near land, how often do they found? And if upon a coast with which they are unacquainted, how careful are they to get a *pilot* that knows and is acquainted with it?

APPLICATION.

Thus watchful and suspicious ought we to be in spiritual concernments. We should study, and be acquainted with Satan's wiles and policy: The Apostle takes it for granted, that christians are not ignorant of his devices, 2 Cor. ii. 11. *The serpent's eye* (as one saith) *would do well in the dove's head:* The devil is a cunning pirate, he puts out false colours, and ordinarily comes up to the christian in the disguise of a friend.

O the manifold deeps and stratagems of Satan, to destroy souls! Though he have no wisdom to do himself good, yet policy enough to do us mischief. He lies in ambush behind our lawful comforts and employments: yet for the most of men, how supine and careless are they, suspecting no danger; Their souls, like *Laish*, dwell carelesly; their senses unguarded. O what an easy prize and conquest doth the devil make of them!

Indeed, if it were with us, as with *Adam* in innocency, or as it was with Christ in the days of his flesh (who by reason of that overflowing fulness of grace that dwelt in him, the purity of his person, and the *hypostacal* union, was secured from the danger of all temptations) the case then were otherwise but we have a *traitor* within, James i. 14 15. As well as a tempter without, 1 Pet. v. 8. " Our adversary the devil goes about as a roaring lion, seeking whom he may devour." And like the beasts of the forest, poor souls, lie down before him, and become his prey. All the sagacity, wit, policy and foresight of some Men, is summoned in to serve their bodies, and secure their fleshy enjoyments.

REFLECTION.

Lord! how doth the care, wisdom, and vigilancy of Men in temporal and external things, condemn my carelesness in the deep and dear concernments of my precious Soul! What care and labour is there to secure a perishing life, liberty, or treasure! When was I thus solicitous for my soul, though its value be inestimable, and its dangers far greater? Self-preservation is one of the deepest principles in nature. There is not the poorest worm or flie, but will shun danger if it can: Yet I am so far from shunning those dangers to which my soul lies continually exposed, that I often run it upon temtations, and voluntarily expose, it to its enemies. I see, Lord, how watchful, jealous and laborious thy people are, what Prayers, tears, and groans, searching of heart, mortification of lusts, guarding of senses: and all accounted too little by them. Have not I a soul to save or lose eternally, as well as they? Yet I cannot deny one fleshly lust, nor withstand one temptation. O, how am I convinced, and condemned; not only by others care and vigilancy, but my own too, in lesser and lower matters!

THE POEM.

"I am the ship, whose bills of lading come
"To more than mans or angels art can sum.
"Rich fraught with mercies, on the Ocean now,
"I float, the dangerous ocean I do plow,
"Storms rise, Rocks threaten, and in every creek
"Pirates and Pickeroens their prizes seek.
"My soul should watch, look out, and use its glass,
"Prevent surprizals timely; but alas!
"Temptations give it chase, it's grappled sure,
"And boarded whilst it thinks it self secure.
"It sleeps like *Jonah*, in the dreadful'st storm,
"Although its case be dangerous and forlorn.
"Lord, rouze my drowsie Soul, lest it should knock
"And split itself upon some dangerous Rock.
"If it of Faith and conscience shipwrack make,
"I am undone for ever: soul awake!
"Till thou arrive in heaven, watch and fear;
"Thou mayst not say till then, the coast is clear."

CHAP. VI.

How small a matter turns a ship about?
Yet we against our conscience stand it out.

OBSERVATION.

IT is just matter of admiration, to see so great a body as a ship is, and when under sail too, before a fresh and strong wind, by which it is carried as the clouds, with marvellous force and speed, yet to be commanded with ease, by so small a thing as the *Helm* is. The scripture takes notice of it as a matter worthy our consideration, Jan. iii. 4. "Behold also the ships, which though they be great, and driven of fierce winds; yet they are turned about with a small helm, whithersoever the Governor listeth." Yea, *Aristotle* himself that Eagle ey'd philosopher, could not give a reason of it, but looked upon it as a very marvellous and wonderful thing.

Aristot. Secunda.
Mecanicon, C. 5.

APPLICATION.

To the same use and office has God designed conscience in man, which being rectified and regulated by the word and spirit of God, is to steer and order his whole conversation. Conscience is as the oracle of God, the judge and determiner of our actions, whether they be good or evil? And it lays the strongest obligations upon the creature to obey its dictates, that is imaginable: for it binds under the reason and consideration of the most absolute and sovereign will of the great God. So that as often as conscience from the word convinceth us of any sin or duty, it lays such a bond upon us to obey it, as no power under heaven can relax or dispense with. Angels cannot do it, much less man; for that would be to exalt themselves above God. Now therefore it is an high and dreadful way of sinning, to oppose and rebel against conscience, when it convinces of sin and duty. Conscience sometimes reasons it out with with men, and shews them the necessity of changing their way and course; arguing it from the clearest and most allowed max-

G

ims of right reason, as well as from the indisputable sovereignty of God.

As for instance: it convinceth their very reason that things of eternal duration are infinitely to be prefered to all momentary and perishing things, Rom. viii. 18. Heb. xi. 26. And it is our duty to chuse them, and make all secular and temporary concernments to stand aside, and give place to them. Yet though men be convinced of this, their stubborn will stands out, and will not yield up itself to the conviction.

Further, It argues from this acknowledged truth, that all the delight and pleasures in this world are but a miserable portion, and that it is the highest folly to adventure an immortal soul for them, Luke ix. 15. Alas! what rememberance is there of them in hell? They are as the waters that pass away. What have they left, of all their mirth and jollity, but a tormenting sting? It convinceth them clearly, also, that in matters of deep concernment it is an high point of wisdom, to apprehend and improve the right seasons and opportunities of them, Prov. x. 5. "He that gathers in summer is a wise son." Eccles. viii. 5. "A wise man's heart discerns both time and judgment. "There is a season to every purpose," Eccles. iii. 1. viz. a nick of time; an happy juncture; when, if a man strikes in, he doth his work effectually, and with much facility: such seasons conscience convinceth the soul of, and often whispers thus in its ear: Now, soul strike in, close with this motion of the spirit, and be happy forever; thou mayest never have such a gale for heaven any more. Now, though these be allowed maxims of reason, and conscience enforce them strongly on the soul, yet cannot it prevail; the proud, stubborn will rebels, and will not be guided by it. See Eph. ii. 3. Job xxxiv. 37. Isa. xlvi. 12. Ezek. ii. 4. Jer. xliv. 16.

REFLECTION.

Ah! Lord, such an heart have I had before thee; thus obstinate, thus rebellious, so uncontroulable by conscience. Many a time hath conscience thus whispered in mine ear, many a time hath it stood in my way, as the angel did in Balaam's, or the cherubims that kept the way of the tree of life with flaming swords turning every way. Thus hath it stood to oppose me in the way of my lusts. How often hath it calmly debated the case with me alone? and how sweetly hath it expostulated with me? How clearly hath it convinced of sin, danger, duty, with strong demonstration? How terrible hath it menaced my soul, and set the point of the threatning at my very breast? And yet my head-strong affections will not be remanded by it. I have obeyed the voice of every lust and temptation, Tit. iii. 3. but conscience hath lost its authority with me. Ah Lord! what a sad condition am I in, both in respect of sin and misery! My sin receives dreadful aggravations, for rebellion and presumption are hereby added to it. I have violated the strongest bonds that ever were laid upon a creature. If my conscience had not thus convinced and warned, the sin had not been so great and crimson-coloured, Jam. iv. 17. Ah! this is to sin with an high hand, Numb. xv. 30. To come near to the great and unpardonable transgression, Psalm xix. 13. O how dreadful a way of sinning is this, with opened eyes! and as my sin is thus out of measure sinful, so my punishment will be out of measure dreadful, if I persist in this rebellion. Lord! thou hast said, Such shall be beaten with many stripes,

Luke xii. 48. Yea, Lord, and if ever my conscience, which by rebellion is now grown silent, should be be in judgment awakened in this life; O! what an hell should I have within me! how would it thunder and roar upon me, and surround me with terrors?

Thy word assures me, that no length of time can wear out of its memory what I have done, Gen. xlii. 21. No violence or force can suppress it, Mat. xxvii. 4, No greatness of power can stifle it; it will take the mightiest monarch by the throat, Exod. x. 16. Dan. v. 6. No musick, pleasures, or delights, can charm it Job xx. 22. O conscience! thou art the sweetest friend, or the dreadfulest enemy in the World; Thy consolations are incomparably sweet and thy terrours insupportable. Ah let me stand it out no longer against conscience; the very ship in which I sail, is a confutation of my madness, that rush greedily into sin against both Reason and conscience, and will not be commanded by it; Surely O my Soul, this will be bitterness in the end.

THE POEM.

 "A ship of greatest burden will obey
 "The rudder; he that sits at helm may sway
 "And guide its motion: If the pilot please,
 "The ship bears up against both Wind and seas,
 "My soul's the ship, affections are its sails,
 "Conscience the rudder. Ah! but Lord what ails
 "My naughty heart, to shuffle in and out,
 "When its convictions bid it tack about?
 "Temptations blow a counter-blast, and drive

"The vessel where they please, tho' conscience strive,
"And by its strong perswasions it would force
"My stubborn will to steer another course.
"Lord, if I run this course, thy Word doth tell
"How quickly I must needs arrive at Hell.
"Then rectifie my conscience, change my will;
"Fan in thy pleasant Gales, my God, and fill
"All my affections; and let nothing carry
"My soul from its due course or make it vary;
"Then if the Pilot's work thou wouldst perform,
"I should bear bravely up against a storm.

CHAP. VII.

*Through many fears and dangers Sea-men run,
Yet all's forgotten when they do return.*

OBSERVATION.

WE have an elegant and lively description of their fears and dangers, Psal. cvii, 25, 26, 27. " He commandeth and raiseth the stormy winds which lifteth up the waves thereof: They mount up to heaven, they go down again to the depths; their soul is melted because of trouble, they reel to and fro, they stagger like a drunken man; they are at their wits end." Or, as it is in the *Hebrew*, *All wisdom is swallowed up.* Suitable to which is that of the poet.

Rector in incerto est, nec quid fugiatave pettve
Invenit, ambiguis ars stupet ipsa malis   Ovid.

The Pilot knows not what to chuse or flee,
Art stands amaz'd in ambiguity.

O what a strange and miraculous deliverance have many seamen had; How often have they yielded themselves for dead men, and verily thought the next sea would have swallowed them up? How earnestly then do they cry for mercy, and like the *Cymbrians,* can pray in a storm, though they regarded it not at other times, Psal. cvii. 28. Jam. i. 5, 6.

APPLICATION.

These dreadful storms do at once discover to us the mighty power of God in raising them, and the abundant goodness of God in preserving poor creatures in them.

1st. The power of God is graciously manifested in raising them: The wind is one of the Lord's wonders, Psal. cvii. 23, 24. " They that go down to the sea, see the works of the Lord, and his (wonders) in the deep: for he commandeth and raiseth the stormy winds." Yea, Psal. cxlvii. 18. God appropriates it as a peculiar work of his; *He causeth* (*His winds to blow*.) Hence, He is said in scripture, *to bring them forth of his treasury,* Job xxxviii. 22. There they are locked up and reserved, not a gust can break forth till he command and call for it to go and execute his pleasure: Yea, He is said to hold them in his fist, Prov. xxx. 4. What is more uncapable of holding than the wind; yet God holds it, Although it be a strong and terrible creature, He controuls and rules it. Yea, the scripture sets forth God, " As riding upon the wings of the wind," Psalm. xviii. 10. It is a borrowed speech from the manner of men, when they would shew their pomp and greatness, ride upon some stately horse or chariot: so the Lord to manifest the greatness of his power, rides upon the wings of the wind, and will be admired in so terrible a creature.

And no less of his glorious power appears in remanding them, than in raising them. The heathens ascribe this power to their god *Aeolus*; but we know this is the *Royalty* and sole Prerogative of the true God, who made heaven and earth; it is he that *makes the storm a calm*, Psal. cvii. 29. And it is He that shifts and changes them from point to point as he pleaseth; for he hath appointed them their circuits, Eccles. i. 6. "The wind goeth towards the south, and turneth about unto the north; it whirleth about continually, and returneth again according to his circuits.

2d. And as we should adore his power in the winds, so ought we to admire his Goodness in preserving men in the height of all their fury and violence. O what a marvellous work of God is here! That men should be kept in a poor weak vessel, upon the wide and stormy ocean, where the wind hath its full stroke upon them, and they are driven before it as a wreck upon the seas; yet, I say, that God should preserve you there, is a work of infinite goodness and power, that those winds which do rend the very earth, mountains and rocks, 1 Kings xix. 11. "Breaks the cedars, yea, the cedars of *Lebanon*, shakes the wilderness and makes the hinds to calve:" which Naturalists say, bring forth with greatest difficulty, Psal. xxix. 5, 8, 9. Surely your preservation in such tempests, is an astonishing work of mercy. O how dreadful is this creature, the wind, sometimes to you? And how doth it make your hearts shake within you; If but a plank spring, or bolt give way, you are all lost. Sometimes the Lord for the magnifying of the riches of his goodness upon you, drives you to such exigencies, that as Paul speaks in a like case, Acts xxvii. 20. *All hope of being saved is taken away*; Nothing but death before your eyes. The Lord commands a wind out of his treasury, bids it go and lift up the terrible waves; lock you in upon the shore, and drive you upon the rocks, so that no art can save you; and then sends you a piece of wreck, or some other means to land you safe: And all this to give you an experiment of his goodness and pity, that you may learn to fear that God, in whose hand your soul and breath is.

And it may be for the present, that your hearts are much affected; conscience works strongly, it smites you for sins formerly committed, such counsels of ministers or relations slighted. Now, saith conscience, God is come in this storm to reckon with thee for these things. But alas, all this is but a morning dew; no sooner is that storm without allayed, but all is quiet within too. How little of the goodness of God abides kindly and effectually upon the heart?

REFLECTION.

How often hath this glorious power and goodness of God passed before me in dreadful storms and tempests at sea? He hath uttered his voice in those stormy winds, and spoken in a terrible manner by them; yet how little have I been affected with it? "The Lord hath his way in the whirlwind, and in the storm," Nah. i. 3. To some he hath walked in ways of Judgment and wrath, sending them down in a moment to hell; but to me in a way of forbearance and mercy. Ah, how often have I been upon the very brink of eternity? had not God shifted or alayed the wind, in a moment; I had gone down into hell. What workings of conscience were at present upon me? And what terrible apprehensions had I then of my eternal condition? What vows did I make in that distress? and how earnestly did I then beg for mercy? but Lord, though thy vows are upon me, yet have I been the same; yea added to, and filled up the measure of my sins. Neither the bonds of mercy thou hast laid upon me, nor the sacred and solemn vows I have laid upon myself, could restrain me from those ways of iniquity, which then appeared so dreadful to me.

Ah Lord, what an heart have I? What love, pity, and goodness have I sinned against? If God had but respited judgment so long what a mercy were it! Sure I am, the damned would account it so; but to give me such a space to repent, Ah what an invaluable mercy is this! And do I thus requite the Lord *Deut.* xxxii. 6. and pervert and abuse his goodness thus? Surely, O my soul, if this be the fruit of all thy preservations, they are rather reservations to some further and sorer judgments. How dreadfully will justice at last avenge the Quarrel of abused Mercy? Josh. xxiv. 20. How grievously did God take it from the *Israelites*, that they provoked him at the Sea, even at the red Sea? Psal. cvi. 7. where God had wrought their deliverance in such a miraculous way. Even thus have I sinned after the similitude of their transgressions; not only against the Laws of God, but against the Love of God. In the last storm he shot off his *Warning-piece*; in the next, he may discharge his *Murdering-piece* against my soul and body. O my soul! hath he given thee "such deliverances as these, and darest thou again break his commandments Ezra.

H

X. 13, 14. "O let me pay the vows that my lips have uttered in my distress, lest the Lord recover his glory from me in a way of judgment."

THE POEM.

"The ship that now sails trim before a wind;
"E're the desired ports it gains, may find
"A tedious passage: Gentle Gales a while
"Do fill its sails, the flattering seas do smile,
"The Face of Heaven is bright, on every side
"The wanton *Porpoise* tumbles on the Tide.
"Into their cabins now the Seamen go,
"And then turn out again, with, *What chear ho?*
"All on a sudden darkened are the skies,
"The lamp of heaven obscur'd, the winds do rise;
"Waves swell like mountains: now their courage flags
"The masts are crackt, the canvas torn to rags.
"The vessel works for life; anon one cries,
"*The main mast's gone by th' Board;* another plies
"The pump, until a third do strike them blank
"With *Sirs, prepare for death we have sprung a plank*
"Now to their knees they go, and on this wise
"They beg for mercy with their loudest cries:
"Lord, save us but this once, and thou shalt see
"What Persons for the future we will be:
"Our former time's mis-spent, but with a vow,
"We will engage, if thou will save us now
"To mend what is amiss. The gracious Lord
"Inclined to pity, takes them at their word;
"The winds into their treasures he doth call,
"Rebukes the stormy sea, and brings them all
"To their desired Haven: once ashore,
"And then their Vows are ne'er remembered more.

"Thus souls are shipwrackt, tho' the bodies live,
"Unless in time thou true Repentance give.

CHAP. VIII.

The navigator shifts his sails, to take,
All winds, but that which for his soul doth make.

OBSERVATION.

THE mariner wants no skill and wisdom to improve several winds, and make them serviceable to his end; a bare side-wind, by his skill in shifting and managing the sails, will serve his turn: He will not lose the advantage of one breath or gale that may be useful to him, I have many times wondered to see two ships sailing in a direct counter motion, by one and the same wind. Their skill and wisdom herein is admirable.

APPLICATION.

Thus prudent and skilful are men in secular and lower matters, and yet how ignorant and unskilful in the great and everlasting affairs of their souls! All their invention, judgement, wit, and memory seem to be pressed for the service of the flesh. They can learn an art quickly, and arrive to a great deal of exactness in it; but in foul-matters, no knowledge at all. They can understand the *Equator, Meridian* and *Horizon*: By the first they can tell the latitude of any place, South or North, measuring it by the degrees in the *Meridian*; by the second they can tell you the longitude of a place, east and west, from the *Meridian*, measuring it by the degrees of the *Equator*: And by the third, they can discern the the divers risings and settings of the Stars. And so in other Arts and sciences, we find men endowed with rare abilities, and singular sagacity. Some have piercing apprehensions, solid judgments, stupendous, memories, rare Invention, and excellent elocution: But put them upon any spiritual supernatural matter, and the weakest christian, even a babe in Christ, shall excel them therein, and give a far better account of Regeneration, the work of grace, the Life of Faith than these can. i. Cor. i. 26. " Not many wise men after the flesh, &c. But God hath chosen the foolish things of this world, &c."

REFLECTION.

How inexcusable then art thou, O my Soul! and how mute and confounded must thou needs stand before the bar of God, in that great day? Thou hadst a *Talent* of natural parts committed to thee, but which way have they been improved? I had an understanding indeed, but it was not sanctified; a Memory, but it was like a Sieve, that let go the corn, and retain'd nothing but husks and chaff; Wit and invention, but alas none to do myself good. Ah! how will these rise in judgment against me, and stop my mouth? What account shall I give for them in that day?

Again: are men (otherwise prudent and skillful) such sots and fools in spiritual things? Then let the poor weak Christian, whose natural parts are blunt and dull, admire the riches of God's free grace to him. O What an astonishing consideration is this? That God should pass by men of the profoundest natural parts, and chuse me, even poor me, whose natural faculties and endowments compared with theirs, are but as Lead to Gold! Thus under the law he past by the Lion and the eagle, and chose the Lamb and Dove. O, how should it make me to advance Grace, as Christ doth upon the same account, Mat. xi. 25. "I thank thee, Father, Lord of Heaven and Earth, that thou hast hid these things from the wise and prudent, and revealed them unto babes." And let it ever be an humbling consideration to me; For who made me to differ? Is not this one principal thing God aims at, in calling such as I am; that boasting may be excluded, and himself alone exalted?

THE POEM.

" One thing doth very much affect my mind,
" To see the Sea men husband every wind;
" With excellent art he shifts the sails and knows
" How to improve the fairest Wind that blows.
" If a direct or fore-right gale he want,
" A side wind serves his turn, tho' ne'r so scant,
" And will not this one day in Judgment rise
" Against your souls? Ah! can you be so wise
" In smaller matters; what, and yet not know
" How to Improve fresh gales of grace that blow?
" Fast moor'd in sin your wind-bound Souls can lie,
" And let these precious gales, rise, blow, and die.

"Sometimes on you affections you may feel
"Such gracious breathings: Ah, but hearts of steel,
"They move you not, nor cause you to relent,
"Though able, like *Elijah's* wind, to rent
"The Rocks asunder: If you do not prize
"Those breathings, other winds will shortly rise,
"And from another quarter; those once gone,
"The next look out for an *Euroclydon*,
"A dreadful storm: how soon no man can tell;
"But when it comes, 'twill blow such souls to hell."

CHAP. IX.

If Sea-men lose a gale, there they may lie:
The Soul when once becalm'd, in sin may die.

OBSERVATION.

SEA-MEN are very watchful to take their opportunity of wind and tide; and it much concerns them so to be: The neglect of a few hours, sometimes loses them their passage, and proves a great detriment to them. They know the wind is an uncertain variable thing? they must take it when they may; they are unwilling to lose one flow, or breath that may be serviceable to them. If a prosperous gale offers, and they not ready, it repents them to lose it, as much as it would repent us to see a vessel of good wine or Beer tapt and run to waste.

APPLICATION.

There are also seasons and gales of grace for our souls; golden opportunities of salvation afforded to men, the neglect of which proves the loss and ruin of souls. God hath given unto men a day of visitation, which he hath *limited*, Heb. iv. 7. and keeps an exact account of every *year, month* and day, that we have enjoyed it, Luke xiii. 7. Jer. xxv. 3. Luke xix. 42. The longest date of it can be but the time of this life : This is our day to work in, John ix. 4. and upon this small wire, the weight of eternity hangs. But sometimes the season of grace is ended before the night of death comes ; the *accepted time* is gone, men frequently out live it, Luke xix. 44. 2. Cor. vi. 2. Or, if the outward means of salvation be continued, yet the spirit many times withdraws from those means, and ceases any more to strive with men ; and then the blessing, power and efficacy is gone from them, and instead thereof a curse seizeth the soul, Heb. vi. 7. 8. and Jer. vi. 30.

Therefore it is a matter of high importance to our souls, to apprehend these seasons. How pathetically doth Christ bewail *Jerusalem*, upon this account ! Luke xix. 42. *O that thou hadst known at least in this thy day, the things of thy peace ! but now they are hid from thine eyes.* If a company of Seamen be set a-shore upon some remote, uninhabited Island, with this advice, to be aboard again exactly at such an hour, else they must be left behind : how doth it concern them to be punctual to their time? The lives of those men depend upon a quarter of an hour. Many a foul hath perished eternally (the Gospel leaving them behind in their sins) because they knew not the time of their visitation.

REFLECTION.

What golden seasons for salvation hast thou enjoyed, O my soul? What Halcyon-days of gospel-light and grace hast thou had? How have the precious gales of grace blown to no purpose upon thee! and the spirit waited and striven with thee in vain? *The kingdom of heaven* (being opened in the gospel-dispensations) *hath suffered violence.* Multitudes have been pressing into it in my days, and I myself have sometimes been *almost persuaded*, and not far from the Kingdom of God: I have gone as far as conviction of sin and misery: yea, I have been carried by the power of the gospel, to resolve and purpose to turn to God, and become a new creature; but sin hath been too subtil and deceitful for me: I see, my resolutions were but as an early cloud, or morning dew; and now my heart is cold and dead again, settled upon its lees: Ah! I have cause to fear and tremble, lest God hath left me under that curse, Rev. xxii. 11. *Let him that is filthy be filthy still.* I fear I am become as that miry place, Ezek. xlvii. 11. that shall not be healed by the streams of the Gospel, but *given to salt*, and cursed into perpetual barrenness. Ah Lord wilt thou leave me so! and shall thy spirit strive no more with me? Then it had been good for me that I had never been born. Ah, if I have trifled out this season and irrecoverably lost it, then I may take up that lamentation, Jer. viii. 20, and say, *My harvest is past, my summer is ended, and I am not saved.*

Every creature knows its time, even the *Turtle, Crane* and *Swallow,* know the time of their coming, Jer. viii. 7. How brutish am I, that have not known the time of my visitation! O thou that art the Lord of life and time, command one gracious season more for me, and make it effectual to me, before I go hence, and be seen no more?

THE POEM.

" A fresh and whisking gale presents to day,
" But now the ship's not ready; winds must stay,
" And wait the sea-men's leisure. Well, to morrow
" They will put out; but then, unto their sorrow,
" That wind is spent, and by that means they gain,
" Perchance a mouth's repentance, if not twain.
" At last another, offers now they're gone;
" But e're they gain their port, the market's done.
" For every work and purpose under heaven,
" A proper time and season God hath given.
" The fowls of heaven, swallow turtle, crane,
" Do apprehend it, and put us to shame.
" Man hath his season too; but that mis-spent,
" There's time enough his folly to repent.
" Eternity's before him, but therein
" No more such golden hours as these have been.
" When these are past away, then you shall find
" That Proverb true, *occasion's bald behind.*
" Delays are dangerous; see that you discern
" Your proper seasons. O that you would learn
" This wisdom from those fools that come too late
" With fruitless cries, when Christ has shut the gate."

CHAP. X.

*By Navigation one place stores another;
And by communion we must help each other.*

OBSERVATION.

THE moſt wiſe God hath ſo diſpenſed his bounty to the ſeveral nations of the world, that one ſtanding in need of anothers commodities, there might be a ſociable commerce and traffick maintained amongſt them all, and all combining in a common league, may by the help of navigation, exhibit mutual ſuccours to each other. The ſtaple commodities proper to each country, I find thus expreſſed by the poet, *Bart. Coll.*

Hence comes our ſugars from *Canary* iſles,
From *Candy* currents, muſkadels, and oyls;
From the *Moluccoes*, ſpices; balſamum
From *Egypt*; odours from *Arabia* come;
From *India* gums, rich drugs and ivory;
From *Syria* mummy; black, red ebony
From burning *Chus*; from *Peru*, pearl and gold;
From *Ruſſia* furs, to keep the rich from cold.
From *Florence* ſilks; from *Spain* fruit, ſaffron, ſacks;
From *Denmark* amber, cordage, firs, and flax;
From *Holland* hops; horſe from the banks of *Rhine*;
From *England* wool: all Lands, as God diſtributes
To the world's treaſure pay their ſundry tributes.

APPLICATION.

Thus hath God diftributed the more rich and precious gifts and graces of his fpirit among his people: Some excelling in one grace, fome in another, tho' every grace, in fome degree, be in them all; even as in *Nature*, tho' there be all the faculties in all, yet fome faculties are in fome more lively and vigorous than in others; fome have a more vigorous eye others a more ready ear, others a more voluble tongue; fo it's in *fpirituals*, *Abraham* excell'd in *Faith*, *Job* in *patience*, *John* in *love*, Thefe were their peculiar excellencies. All the elect veffels are not of one quantity; yet even thofe that excel others in fome particular grace, come fhort in other refpects of thofe they fo excelled in the former, and may be much improv'd by converfe with fuch as in fome refpects are much below them. The folid, wife, and judicious chriftian may want that livelinefs of affections, and tendernefs of heart, that appears in the weak; and one that excels in gifts and utterance, may learn humility from the very babes in Chrift.

And one principal reafon of this different diftribution, is to maintain fellowfhip among them all, 1 Cor. xii. 21. "The head cannot fay to the feet I have no need of you." As in a family, where there is much bufinefs to be done, even the little children bear a part, according to their ftrength, Jer. vii. 18: "The children gather wood the fathers kindle the fire, the women knead the dough." So in the family of Chrift, the weakeft chriftian is ferviceable to the ftrong.

There be precious treasures in these earthen vessels, for which we should trade by mutual communion. The preciousness of the treasure, should draw out our desires and endeavours after it; and the consideration of the brittleness of those vessels in which they are kept, should cause us to be the more expeditious in our trading with them, and make the quicker returns: For when those vessels (I mean the bodies of the saints) are broken by death, there is no more to be gotten out of them. That treasure of grace which made them such profitable, pleasant, and desirable companions on earth, then ascends with them into heaven, where every grace receives its adolesence and perfection: And then though they be ten thousand times more excellent and delightful than ever they were on earth, yet we can have no more communion with them, till we come to glory ourselves. Now therefore it behoves us to be enriching ourselves by communication of what God hath dropt into us, and improvement of them; as one well notes.

Mr. Gurnal. We should do by saints, as we use to do by some choice book lent us for a few days, we should fix in our memories, or transcribe all the choice notions we meet with in it, that they may be our own when the book is called for, and we can have it no longer by us.

REFLECTION.

Lord, how short do I come of my duty in communicating to, or receiving good by others! My soul is either empty and barren, or if there be any treasure in it, yet it is but as a treasure locked up in some chest, whose key is lost, when it should be opened for the use of others. Ah Lord! I have sinned greatly, not only by vain words, but sinful silence, I have been of little use in the world.

How little also have I gotten by communion with others? Some, it may be, that are of my own *size* or *judgment*, or that I am otherwise obliged to, I can delight to converse with: But O, where is that largeness of heart, and general delight I should have to, and in all thy people? How many of my old dear acquaintance are now in heaven, whose tongues were as *choice silver*, while they were here, Prov. x. 20. And blessed souls, how communicative were they of what thou gavest them? O what an improvement had I made of my talent this way, had I been diligent! Lord pardon my neglect of those sweet and blessed advantages. O let all my delight be in thy saints, who are the *excellent of the earth*. Let me never go out of their company, without an heart more warmed, quickned, and enlarged, than when I came amongst them.

THE POEM.

"To several nations God doth so distribute
"His bounty, that each one must pay a tribute
"Unto each other. *Europe* cannot vaunt,
"And say, of *Africa* I have no want.
"*America* and *Asia* need not strive,
"Which of itself can best subsist and live.
"Each countries want, in something, doth maintain

"Commerce betwixt them all. Such is the aim
"And end of God, who doth dispense and give
"More grace to some, their brethren to relieve.
"This makes the *sun* ten thousand times more bright
"Because it is diffusive of its light,
"Its beams are gilded gloriously; but then
"This property doth gild them o'er again.
"Should sun, moon, stars, impropriate all their light,
"What dismal darkness would the world benight?
"On this account men hate the vermin brood,
"Because they take in much, but do no good.
"What harm, if I at yours, my candle light:
"Except thereby, I make your room more bright.
"He that, by pumping, sucks and draws the spring,
"New streams, and sweeter, to that well doth bring.
"Grace is a treasure in an earthen pot;
"When death hath dasht it, no more can be got
"Out of that vessel: Then, while it is whole,
"Get out the treasure to enrich your soul."

CHAP. XI.

The rocks abide, though seas against them rage,
So shall the Church, which is God's heritage.

OBSERVATION.

THE rocks, though situate in the boisterous and tempestuous ocean, yet abide firm and immovable from age to age: The impetuous waves dash against them with great violence, but cannot remove them out of their place. And although sometimes they wash over them, and make them to disappear, yet there they remain fixt and impregnable.

APPLICATION.

This is a lively emblem of the condition of the church, amidst all dangers and oppositions wherewith it is encountred and and assaulted in this world. These *metaphorical* waves roar and beat with violence against it, but with as little success as the sea against the rock, Mat. xvi. 18. "Upon this rock will I build my church, and the (gates) of hell shall not prevail against it." The gates of hell are the power and policy of hell; for it is convinced to be an allusive speech to the gates of the *Jews* wherein their ammunition for war was lodged, which also were the seats of judicature, there sate the judges: but yet, these gates of hell shall not prevail. Nay, this rock is not only invincible in the midst of their violence, but also breaks all that dash against it, Zech. xii. 3. "In that day I will make *Jerusalem* a burdensome stone for all people: all that burden themselves with it, shall be cut in pieces, though all the people of the earth be gathered together, against it." An allusion to one that essays to roll some great stone against the hill, which at last returns upon him, and crushes him to pieces.

And the reason why it is thus firm and impregnable, is not from itself; for alas, so considered, it is weak and obnoxious to ruin; but from the almighty power of God, which guards and preserves it day and night, Psal. xlvi. 5, 6. "God is in the midst of her, she shall not be moved: God shall help her, and that right early." Vatab. *Dum aspicit mane.* When the morning appears: Which notes (saith *Calvin*) God's assiduous and constant help and succour, which is extended in all dangers; as constantly as the sun rises. And this assiduous succour to his people, and their great security thereby, is set forth in the scriptures by a pleasant variety of metaphors and emblems, Zech. ii. 5. "I (saith the Lord) will be a wall of fire round about it. Some think this phrase alludes to the *Cherubims*, that kept the way of the tree of life with flaming swords: Others, to the fiery chariots round about Datham, where Elisha was: but most think it to be an allusion to an ancient custom of travellers in the desarts; who to prevent the assaults of wild beasts in the night, made a *Circular fire* round about them, which was as a wall to them. Thus will God be to his people, *a wall of fire*, which none can scale. So Exod. iii, 3, 4, 5. We have an excellent emblem of the churches low and dangerous condition, and admirable preservation. You have here, both a *marvel* and a *mystery:* The marvel was to see a bush all on fire and yet not consumed. The mystery is this: the bush represented the sad condition of the church in Egypt; the fire flaming upon it, the grievious afflictions, troubles, and bondage it was in there; the remaining of the bush unconsumed, the strange and admirable preservation of the church in those troubles. It lived there as the three noble *Jews*, untouched in the midst of a burning fiery furnace: And the *angel of the Lord* in a flame of fire in the midst of the bush, was nothing elfe but the *Lord Jefus Chrift*, powerfully and gracioufly prefent with his people, amidft all their dangers and fufferings. The Lord is exceeding tender over them, and jealous for them, as that expreffion imports, Zech. ii. 8. " He that touches you, touches the apple of mine eye." He that ftrikes at them, ftrikes at the face of God; and at the moft excellent part of the face, the eye; and at the moft tender and precious part of the eye the apple of the eye. And yet (as a learned modern oberves) this people of whom he ufes this tener and dear expreffion, were none of the beft of Ifrael neither; but the refidue that ftaid behind in *Babylon*, when their brethern were gone to rebuild the temple; and yet over thefe, is he as tender, as a man is over his eye.

REFLECTION.

And is the fecurity of the church fo great! and its prefervation fo admirable, amidft all ftorms and tempefts! then, why art thou fo prone and fubject to defpond, O my foul, in the day of *Sions* trouble? Senfible thou waft, and oughteft to be; but no reafon to hang down the head through difcouragement, much lefs to forfake *Sion* in her diftrefs, for fear of being ruined with her.

What *David* fpake to *Abiathar*, 1 Sam. xxii. 23. that may *Zion* fpeak to all her fons and daughters in all their diftreffes: " Though he that feeketh thy life, feeketh mine alfo; yet with me fhalt thou be in fafeguard. God hath entailed great falvation and deliverance upon *Sion*; and bleffed are all her friends and favourites; the rock of ages is it's defence. Fear not therefore, O my foul, though the hills be removed out of their place, and cast into the midst of the sea. O let my faith triumph, and my heart rejoice upon this ground of comfort. I see the same rocks now, and in the same place and condition they were many years ago. Though they have endured many storms, yet there they abide; and so shall *Sion*, when the proud waves have spent their fury and rage against it.

THE POEM.

" *Mesopotamia*, situate in the seas,
May represent the church, or if you please,
A rock, o'er which the waves do wash and swill,
May figure it; chuse either, which you will.
Winds strive upon those seas, and make a noise,
The lofty waves sometimes lift up their voice,
And swelling high, successively do beat
With violence against it, then retreat.
They break themselves, but it abides their shock;
And when their rage is spent, there stands the rock.
Then they are out, that do affirm and vote,
Peace, pomp, and splendour is the churches *Note*.
And they deserve no less reproof, that are
In *Zion's* troubles ready to despair.
This rock amidst far stronger rocks do lie,
Which are its fence; so *deep*, *so thick*, *so high*,
They can't be *batter'd scal'd*, or *undermin'd*:
And these, environ'd by them, daily find
Their bread ascertain'd; waters too secur'd
Then shout and sing, ye that are thus immur'd:

CHAP. XII.

What dangers run they for a little gains,
Who for their souls, would ne'er take half the pains!

HOW exceeding solicitous and adventurous are seamen for a small portion of the world? How prodigal of strength and life for it? They will run to the ends of the earth, engage in a thousand dangers, upon the hopes and probability of getting a small estate. *Per mare, per terras, per mille pericula current.* Hopes of gain makes them willing to adventure their liberty, yea, their life; and encourages them to endure heat, cold, and hunger, and a thousand streights and difficulties, to which they are frequently exposed.

APPLICATION.

How hot and eager are mens affections after the world? And how remiss and cold toward things eternal? They are careful, and troubled about many things, but seldom mind the great and necessary matters, Luke x. 41. They can rise early, go to bed late, eat the bread of carefulness: But when did they so deny themselves for their poor souls? Their heads are full of designs and projects to get or advance an estate: "We will go into such a city, continue there a year, and buy and sell, and get gain," James iv. 13. This is the *to ergon*, the *master-design*, which engrosseth all their time, studies and contrivances. The will hath past a decree for it, the heart and affections are fully let out to it, *They will be rich*, 1 Tim. vi. 9. This decree of the will, the spirit of God takes deep notice of it; and indeed it is the clearest and fullest discovery of man's portion and condition: For, look what is highest in the estimation, first and last in the thoughts, and upon which we spend our treasure, Mat. vi. 20, 21, The heads and hearts of saints are full of solicitous cares and fears about their spiritual condition: The great design they drive on, to which all other things are but (*parraga*,) things on the by, is to make sure their calling and election. This is the ? (*pondus*) the weight and byas of their spirit: if their hearts stray and wander after any other thing, this reduces them again.

REFLECTION.

Lord, this hath been my manner from my youth, may the carnal minded men say; I have been labouring for the meat that perisheth; disquieting myself in vain, full of designs and projects for the world, and unwearied in my endeavours to compass an earthly treasure; yet therein I have either been checkt and disappointed by providence; or if I have obtained, yet I am no sooner come to enjoy that content and comfort I promised myself in it, but I am ready to leave it all, to be stript out of it by death, and in that day all my thoughts perish. But in the mean time, what have I done for my soul? When did I ever break a night's sleep, or deny and pinch myself for it? Ah fool that I am! to nourish and pamper a vile body, which must shortly lie under the clods and become a loathsome carcase; and in the mean time, neglect and undo my poor soul, which partakes of the nature of angels, and must live for ever. I have kept others' vineyards, but mine own vineyard I have not kept: I have been a perpetual drudge and slave to the world; in a worse condition hath my soul been, than others that are condemned to the mines. Lord change my treasure, and change my heart: O let it suffice that I been thus long labouring in the fire, for very vanity. Now gather up my heart and affections in thyself, and let my great design now be, to secure a special interest in thy blessed self, that I may once say, To me to live is Christ.

THE POEM.

" The face of man imprest and stampt on Gold,
" With crown and royal scepters we behold.
" No wonder that an humane face it gains,
" Since head, heart, soul and body it obtains.
" Nor is it strange a scepter it should have,
" That to its yoke the world doth so enslave,
" Charm'd with its chinking note, away they go
" Like eagles to the carcase, ride and row.
" Thro' worlds of hazards foolish creatures run,
" That into its embraces they may come.
" Poor *Indians* in the mines my heart condoles,
" But seldom turns aside to pity souls,
" Which are the slaves indeed, that toil and spend

"Themselves upon its service, Surely, friend,
"They are but sextons to prepare and make
"Thy grave within those mines, whence they do take
"And dig their ore. Ah! many souls, I fear,
"Whose bodies live, yet lie entombed there.
"Is gold so tempting to you? Lo, Christ stands,
"With length of days, and riches in his hand.
"Gold in the fire tried he freely proffers;
"But few regard or take those golden offers.

CHAP. XIII.

Millions of creatures in the seas are fed:
Why then are saints in doubt of daily bread?

OBSERVATION.

THERE are multitudes of living creatures in the sea. The *Psalmist* saith, there are in it "Things creeping innumerable, both small and great beasts," Psal. civ. 25. And we read, Gen. i. 20. That when God blessed the waters he said, let the waters bring forth abundantly, both fish and fowl, that move in it, and fly above it. Yet all those multitudes of fish and fowl, both in sea and land, are cared and provided for, Psal. cxlv. 15, 16. "Thou givest them their meat in due season; thou openest thy hand, and satisfiest the desire of every living thing."

APPLICATION.

If God takes care for the fishes of the sea, and fowls of the air, much more will he care and provide for those that fear him. " When the poor and needy seeketh water, and there is none; and their tongue faileth for thirst; I the Lord will hear them, I the God of *Israel* will not forsake them, *Isa.* xli. 17. Take no thought for your life (*faith the Lord*) what ye shall eat, or what ye shall drink; or for the body what ye shall put on:" Which he backs with an argument from God's providence over the creature, and enforceth it with a (*much rather*) upon them, Mat. vi. 25, 31. God would have his people without *carefulness* (*i. e.*) anxious care, 1 Cor. vii. 32. " And to cast their care upon him, for he careth for them," 1 Pet. v. 7. There be two main arguments suggested in the gospel, to quiet and satisfie the hearts of saints in this particular: The one is, that the gift of Jesus Christ amounts to more than all these things come to? Yea, in bestowing him, he has given that which virtually and eminently comprehends all these inferiour mercies in it, Rom. 8. 32. " He that spared not his own Son but delivered him up for us all? how, shall he not with him freely give us all things? And 1 Cor. iii. 22. All things are yours, and ye are Christ's, and Christ is God's." Another argument is, that God gives these temporal things to those he never gave his Christ unto, and therefore there is no great matter in them: Yea, to those, which in a little while are to be thruſt into hell, Pſal. xvii. 14. Now, if God clothe and feed his enemies, if (to allude to that, Luke xii. 28.) He clothes this graſs, which to day is in its pride and glory in the field, and tomorrow is caſt into the oven, into hell. How much more will he cloath and provide for you that are ſaints?

This God that feeds all the creatures, is your father, and a father that never dies; and therefore you ſhall not be as expoſed orphans, that are the children of ſuch a father. "For he hath ſaid, I will never leave you, nor forſake you," Heb. xiii. 5. I have read of a good woman, that in all wants and diſtreſſes, was wont to encourage herſelf with that word, 2 Sam. xxii. 47. *The Lord liveth*. But one time being in a deep diſtreſs, and forgetting that conſolation, one of her little children came to her and ſaid, *Mother, why weep ye ſo? What is God dead now?* Which words from a child, ſhamed her out of her unbelieving fears, and quickly brought her ſpirit to reſt. O Saint! whilſt God lives, thou canſt not want what is good for thee.

How ſweet a life might chriſtians live, could they but bring their hearts to a full ſubjection to the diſpoſing will of God! to be content not only with what he commands and approves, but alſo with what he allots and appoints. It was a ſweet reply, that a gracious woman once made upon her death-bed, to a friend that aſked her whether ſhe were more willing to live or die? She anſwer'd, I am pleas'd with what God pleaſeth. Yea, ſaid her friend, but if God ſhould refer it to you, which would you chuſe? Truly, (*faith ſhe*) if God ſhould refer it to me, I would refer it to him again. Ah bleſt life, when the will is ſwallow'd up in the will of God, and the heart at reſt in his care and love, and pleaſed with all his appointments!

REFLECTION.

I remember my fault this day, may many a gracious foul say. Ah how faithless and distrustful have I been notwithstanding the great security God hath given to my faith, both in his word and works! O my soul, thou hast greatly sinned therein, and dishonoured thy Father! I have been worse to my Father, than my children are to me. They trouble not their thoughts with what they shall eat or drink, or put on, but trust to my care and provision for that: Yet I cannot trust my Father, though I have have ten thousand times more reason so to do, than they have to trust me, Mat. 7. 21. Surely, unless I were jealous of my Father's affection, I could not be so dubious of his provision for me. Ah, I should rather wonder that I have so much, than repine that I have no more. I should rather have been troubled that I have done no more for God, than that I have received no more from God. I have not proclaimed it to the world by my conversation, that I have found a sufficiency in him alone, as the saints have done, Hab. iii. 17, 18. How have I debased the faithfulness and all sufficiency of God, and magnified these earthly trifles, by my anxiety about them? Had I had more faith, a light purse would not have made such an heavy heart. Lord how often hast thou convinced me of this folly, and put me to the blush, when thou hast confuted my unbelief; so that I have resolved never to distrust thee more, and yet new exigencies renew this corruption? How contradictory also hath my heart and my prayers been? I pray for them conditionally, and with submission to thy will: I must have them; yet this hath been the language of my heart and life. O convince me of this folly.

THE POEM.

" Variety of curious fish are caught
" Out of the sea, and to our tables brought;
" We pick the choicest bits, and then we say,
" We are suffic'd; come, now take away.
" The table's voided, you have done; but fain
" I would persuade to have it brought again.
" The sweetest bit of all remains behind
" Which through your want of skill, you could not find.
" A bit for faith, have you not found it? Then
" I have made but half a meal; come taste agen,
" Hast thou considered (O my soul) that hand
" Which feeds those multitudes in sea and land?
" A double mercy in it thou should see;
" It fed them first, and then with them fed thee.
" Food in the waters we should think were scant
" For such a multitude, yet none do want.
" What numerous flocks of birds above me fly?
" When saw I one, through want fall down and die?
" They gather what his hand to them doth bring,
" Tho' but a worm, and at that feast can sing.
" How full a table doth my Father keep?
" Blush then, my naughty heart, repent and weep;
" How faithless and distrustful hast thou been,
" Although his care and love thou oft hast seen?
" Thus in a single dish you have a feast,
" Your first and second course, the last the best,

CHAP. XIV.

Sea-waters drained through the earth are sweet;
So are th' afflictions which God's people meet.

OBSERVATION.

THE waters of the sea in themselves, are brackish and unpleasant, yet being exhaled by the sun, and condensed into clouds, they fall down in pleasant showers: or if drained through the earth, their property is thereby altered; and that which was so salt in the sea, becomes exceeding sweet and pleasant in the springs. This we find by constant experience, the sweetest crystal spring came from the sea, Eccles. i. 7.

APPLICATION.

Afflictions in themselves are evil, Amos ii. 6. Very bitter and unpleasant. See Heb. xii. xi. Yet not morally and intrinsically evil, as sin is; for if so, the holy God would never own it for his own act, as he doth, Mic. iii. 2. but always disclaimeth sin, Jam. i. 3. Besides, if it were so evil, it could in no case, or respect, be the object of our election and desire; as in some cases it ought to be, Heb. xi. xxv. But it is evil, as it is the fruit of sin, and grievous unto sense, Heb. xiv. 11. But though it be thus brackish and unpleasant in itself, yet passing through Christ, and the covenant, it loses that ungrateful property, and becomes pleasant in the fruits and effects thereof, unto believers, Heb. xii. 11.

Yea, such are the blessed fruits thereof, that they are to account it all joy, when they fall into divers afflictions, Jam. i. 2. *David* could bless God, that he was afflicted; and many a saint hath done the like. A good woman once compared her afflictions to her children: "For *(saith she)* they put me in pain in bearing them; yet as I know not which child, so neither which affliction I could be without."

Sometimes the Lord sanctifies affliction to discover the corruption that is in the heart, Deut. viii. 2. It is a furnace to shew the dross. Ah! when a sharp affliction comes, then the pride, impatiency, and unbelief of the heart appears. *Matura vexata prodit seipsam.* When the water is stirred, then the mud and filthy sediment that lay at the bottom rises. Little (saith the afflicted soul) did I think, there had been in me that pride, self-love, distrust of God, carnal fear, and unbelief, as I now find. O where is my patience, my faith, my glory in tribulation? I could not have imagined the sight of death would have so appalled me, the loss of outward things so have pierced me. Now what a blessed thing is this, to have the heart thus discovered?

Again: Sanctified afflictions discover the emptiness and vanity of the creature. Now the Lord hath stained its pride, and vailed its tempting splendour, by this or that affliction; and the soul sees what an empty, shallow, deceitful thing it is. The world (as one hath truly observed) is then only great in our eyes when we are full of sense and self: But now affliction makes us more spiritual, and then it is nothing. It drives them nearer to God, makes them see the necessity of the life of faith, with multitudes of other benefits.

But yet these sweet fruits of affliction do not naturally, and of their own accord, spring from it: No, we may as well look for *grapes* from *thorns*, or *figs* from *thistles*, as for such fruits from affliction, till Christ's sanctifying hand and art have past upon them.

The reason why they become thus sweet and pleasant (as I noted before) is, because they run now into another channel; Jesus Christ hath removed them from mount Ebel to Gerezim; they are no more the effects of vindictive wrath, but paternal chastisement. And (as Mr. Case well notes) " A teaching affliction is to the saints, the result of all the offices of Jesus Christ. As a king, he chastens; as a prophet, he teacheth, viz. by chastening; and as a priest, he hath purchased this grace of the father, that the dry rod might blossom, and bear fruit." Behold then, a sanctified affliction is a cup, whereinto Jesus christ hath wrung and prest the juice and virtue of all his mediatory offices. Surely. that must be a cup of generous, royal wine, like that in the supper, a cup of blessing to the people of God.

Correction, Instruction, page 182.

REFLECTION.

Hence may the unsanctified soul draw matter of fear and trouble, even from its unsanctified troubles. And thus it may reflect upon itself; O my soul, what good hast thou gotten by all, or any of thy afflictions? God's rod hath been dumb to thee, or thou deaf to it. I have not learned one holy Instruction from it: My troubles have left me the same, or worse than they found me; my heart was proud, earthly, and vain before, and so it remains still: They have not purged out, but only given vent to the pride, murmur, and atheism of my heart. I have been in my afflictions, as that wicked Ahaz was in his, 2 Chron. xxviii. 22. "*Who in the midst of his distress, yet trespassed more and more against the Lord.*" When I have been in storms at sea, or troubles at home, my soul within me hath been as a raging sea, casting up mire and dirt. Surely this rod is not the rod of God's children. I have proved but dross in the furnace, and I fear the Lord will put me away as dross, as he threatens to do by the wicked, Psal. cxix. 119.

Hence also should gracious souls draw much encouragement and comfort amidst all their troubles. O these are the fruits of God's fatherly love to me! Why should I fear in the day of evil? or tremble any more at affliction? though they seem as a serpent at a distance, yet are they a rod in hand. O blessed be that skilful and gracious hand, that makes the rod the dry rod to blossom, and bear such precious fruit.

Lord! what a mystery of love lies in this dispensation! That sin which first brought affliction into the world, is now itself carried out of the world by affliction, Rom. v. 12. Isa. vii. 9. O what can frustrate my salvation, when those very things that seem most to oppose it, are made subservient to it; and contrary to their own nature do promote and further it?

THE POEM.

" 'Tis strange to hear what different censures fall
" Upon the same affliction ; some do call
" Their troubles sweet, some bitter ; others meet
" Them both mid-way, and call them bitter sweet.
" But here's the question still I fain would see,
" Why sweet to him and bitter unto me ?
" Thou drink'st them dregs and all, but others fin'd
" Their troubles sweet, because to them refin'd,
" And sanctifi'd ; which difference is best,
" By such apt Similies as these exprest.
" From salt and brackish seas fumes rise and fly
" Which into clouds condens'd obscure the skie,
" Their property there alter'd in few hours
" Those brackish fumes fall down in pleasant showers
" Or as the dregs of wine and beer distill'd
" By limbeck, with ingredients, doth yield
" A cordial water, though the lees were bitter,
" From whence the chymist did extract such liquor.
" Then marvel not that one can kiss that rod,
" Which makes another to blaspheme his God.
" O get your troubles sweet'ned and refin'd
" Or else they'll leave bitter effects behind.
" Saints troubles are a cord, let down by love,
" To pully up their hearts to things above.

CHAP. XV.

Seas within their bounds the Lord contains;
He also men and devils holds in chains.

OBSERVATION.

IT is a wonderful work of God; to limit and bound such a vast and furious creature, as the sea; which, according to the judgment of many learned men, is higher than the earth; and that it hath a propension to overflow it, is evident, both from its nature and motion; were it not, that the great God had laid his law upon it. And this is a work wherein the Lord glories, and will be admired, Psal. civ. 9. "Thou hast set a bound that they may not pass over, that they turn not again to cover the earth." Which it is clear they would do, were they not thus limited. So Job. xxxviii. 8, 10, 11. "Who shut up the seas with doors, when it brake forth, as if it had issued out of the womb? I brake up for it my decreed place, and set bars and doors, and said, hitherto shalt thou come, but no further; and here shall thy proud waves be staid.

APPLICATION.

And no less is the glorious power and mercy of God discovered in bridling the rage and fury of Satan and his instruments, that they break not in upon the inheritance of the Lord, and destroy it. "Surely, the wrath of man shall praise thee, the remainder of wrath shalt thou restrain." Psal. lxxvi. 10. By which it is more than hinted, that there is a world of rage and malice in the hearts of wicked men, which fain would, but cannot vent itself, because the Lord restrains, or as the Hebrew, *Girds it up.* Satan is the envious one, and his rage is great against the people of God, Rev. xii. 12. But God holds him and all his instruments in a chain of providence; and it is well for God's people, that it is so.

They are limited as the sea, and so the Lord in a providential way speaks to them, hitherto shall you come, and no further. Sometimes he ties them up so short, that they cannot touch his people, though they have the greatest opportunities and advantages, Psal. cv, 12, 13, 14, 15. "When they were but a few men in number, yea, very few, and strangers in it; when they went from one nation to another, from one kingdom to another people: He suffered no man to do them wrong; yea, he reproved kings for their sakes, saying, touth not mine anointed, and do my prophets no harm." And sometimes he permits them to touch and trouble his people, but then sets bounds and limits to them, beyond which they must not pass. That is a pregnant text to this purpose, "Revel. ii. 10. Behold, the devil shall cast some of you into prison, that you may be tried, and ye shall have tribulation ten days."

Here are four remarkable limitations, upon satan and his agents, in reference to the people of God: A limitation as to the persons, not all, but some: A limitation of the punishment, a prison, not a grave, not hell: A limitation upon them as to the end; for trial, not ruin: And lastly as to the *duration*, not as long as they please, but ten days.

REFLECTION.

O my soul, what marrow and fatness, comfort, and consolation, mayest thou suck from the breast of this truth, in the darkest day of trouble? Thou seest how the flowing sea drives to overwhelm the earth. Who has arrested it in its course, and stopt its violence! Who has confined it to its place? Certainly none other but the Lord. When I see it threaten the shore with its proud, furious, and insulting waves, I wonder it doth not swallow up all: But I see it no sooner touch the sands, which God hath made its bounds, but it retires, and as it were with a kind of submission, respects those limits which God hath set it.

Thus the fiercest element is represt by the feeblest things: Thou seest also, how full of wrath and fury wicked men are, how they rage like the troubled sea, and threaten to overwhelm *thee, and all

---

* See the Turk's Letter to the Emperor of Germany, lately published by Authority.

the Lord's inheritance: and then the floods of ungodly men make thee afraid, yet are they restrained by an invisible gracious hand, that they cannot execute their purpose, nor perform their enterprize. How full of devils and devilized men, is this lower world? Yet in the midst of them all hast thou hitherto been preserved. O my soul admire and adore that glorious power of God, by which thou art kept unto salvation. Is not the preservation of a saint in the midst of such hosts of enemies as great a miracle, though not so sensible, as the preservation of those three noble Jews in the midst of the fiery furnace, or Daniel in the den of lions? For there is as strong a propension in Satan, and wicked men, to destroy the saints; as in the fire to burn, or a lion to devour. O then let me chearfully address myself to the faithful discharge of my duty, and stand no longer in a slavish fear of creatures, who can have no power against me, but what is given them from above, John xix. 11. And no more shall be given than shall turn to the glory of God, Psal. lxxvi. 10. and the advantage of my soul, Rom. viii. 28.

THE POEM.

"This world's a forest, where from day to day,
"Bears, wolves, and lions range and seek their prey,
"Amidst them all poor harmless Lambs are fed,
"And by their very dens in safety led.
"They roar upon us, but are held in chains:
"Our Shepherd, is their keeper, he maintains

"Our lot. Why then should we so trembling stand?
"We meet them, true, but in their keeper's hand.
"He that to raging seas such bounds hath put
"The mouths of ravenous beast can also shut.
"Sleep in the woods, poor lambs yourselves repose
"Upon his care, whose eyes do never close.
"If unbelief in you don't loose their chain,
"Fear not their struggling, that's but all in vain.
"If God can check the waves by smallest Sand
"A twined thread may hold these in his hand.
"Shun sin, keep close to Christ; for other evils
"You need not fear, tho' compast round with devils.

CHAP. XVI.

*To sea without a compass none dare go;
Our course without the word is even so.*

OBSERVATION.

OF how great use and necessity is the compass to sea men? Though they can coast a little way by the shore, yet they dare not venture far into the ocean without it. It is their guide, and directs and shapes their course for them: And if by the violence of wind and weather they are driven beside their due course, yet by the help of this, they are reduced and brought to rights again. It is wonderful to consider, how by the help of this guide they can run in a direct line many hundred leagues, and at last fall right with the smallest island; which is in the ocean, comparatively, but as the head of a small pin upon a table.

APPLICATION.

What the compass, and all other mathematical instruments are to the navigator, that and much more is the word of God to us in our course to heaven. This is our compass to steer our course by, and it is truly touched; he that orders his conversation by it, shall safely arrive in heaven at last. Gal. vi. 16. *As many as walk according to this rule, peace be on them and mercy.*

This word is as necessary to us in our way to glory, as a lamp or lanthorn is in a dark night, Psal. cxix. 105. That is a light shining in a dark place, till the day dawn, and the day-star arise in our hearts, 2 Pet. i. 19. If any that profess to know it and own it as a rule, miss heaven at last; let them not blame the word for misguiding them, but their own negligent and deceitful hearts, that shuffle in and out, and shape not their course and conversation according to its prescriptions.

What blame can you lay upon the compass, if you steer not exactly by it? How many are there, that neglecting this rule, will coast it to heaven by their own reason? No wonder such fall short and perish in the way. This is a faithful guide, and brings all that follow it to the blessed end, " *Thou shall guide me with thy counsel, and afterwards receive me to glory,* Psal. lxxiii. 24. The whole hundredth and ninteenth Psalm is spent in commendation of its transcendent excellency and usefulness. *Luther* professt, that he prized it so highly, that he would not take the whole world in exchange for one leaf of it. Lay but this rule before you; and walk accurately by it; and you cannot be out of your way to heaven, Psal. cxix. 30. *I have chosen the way of truth, (or the true way;) thy judgment have I laid before me.* Some indeed have opened their detracting blasphemous mouths against it; as Julian, that cursed apostate, who feared not to say, there was as good matter in Phocillides as in Solomon, in Pindarus' Odes, as in David's Psalms.

And the papists generally slight it, making it a lame imperfect rule; yea, making their own traditions the touchstone of doctrines, and foundation of faith. Montanus tells us, that although the apostle would have sermons and service celebrated in a known tongue, yet the church, for very good cause, hath otherwise ordered it. Gilford called it, the mother of heresies. Bonner's chaplain judged it worthy to be burnt as a strange doctrine. They set up their inventions above it, and frequently come in with a *Non obstante* against Christ's institutions. And thus do they make it void, or, as the word *anateilontes* signifies, Mat. xv. 6. Unlord it and take away its authority as a rule. But those that have thus slighted it, and followed the by-paths unto which their corrupt hearts have led them, they take not hold of the paths of life, and are now in the depths of hell. All other lights, to which men pretend, in the neglect of this, are but false fires; that will lead men into the pits and bogs of destruction at last.

REFLECTION.

And is thy word a compass, to direct my course to glory? O where am I then like to arrive at last, that in all my course have neglected it, and steered according to the counsel of my own heart! Lord, I have not made thy word the man of my counsel, but consulted with flesh and blood; I have not enquired at this oracle, nor studied it, and made it the guide of my way; but walked after the sight of my eyes, and the lust of my heart. Whither Lord can I come at last, but to hell, after this rate and reckoning? Some have slighted thy word professedly, and I have slighted it practically. I have a poor soul embarqued for eternity, it is now floating on a dangerous ocean, rocks and sands on every side, and I go a drift before every wind of temptation, and know not where I am. Ah Lord, convince me of the danger of this condition. O convince me of my ignorance in thy word, and the fatal consequence and issue thereof. Lord, let me now resolve to study, prize, and obey it; hide it in my heart, that I may not sin against it: Open my understanding, that I may understand the scriptures: Open my heart to entertain it in love. O thou that hast been so gracious to give a perfect rule, give me also a perfect heart to walk by that rule to glory!

THE POEM.

" This world's a sea, wherein a numerous fleet
" Of ships are under sail. Here you shall meet
" Of every rate and size; Frigates, Galleons,
" The nimble ketches and small pickeroons:
" Some bound to this port, some where winds and weather

" Will drive them, they are bound they know not whither.
" Some steer away for heaven, some for hell;
" To which some steer, themselves can hardly tell.
" The winds do shape their course, which tho' it blow
" From any point, before it they must go.
" They are directed by the wind and tide,
" That have no compass to direct and guide:
" For want of this, must run themselves a ground,
" Brave ships are cast away, poor souls are drown'd.
" Thy word our compass is to guide our way
" To glory; it reduces such as stray.
" Lord, let thy word dwell richly in my heart,
" And make me skilful in this heavenly art,
" O let me understand and be so wise,
" To know upon what point my country lies.
" And having set my course directly thither,
" Great God preserve me in the foulest weather.
" By reason some will coast it: but I fear
" Such coasters never will drop anchor there.
" Thy word is truly toucht, and still directs
" A proper course which my base heart neglects.
" Lord touch mine iron heart, and make it stand
" Pointing to thee, its loadstone to that land
" Of Rest above. Let every tempest drive
" My soul, where it would rather be than live."

CHAP. XVII.

*Look as the Sea by turns doth ebb and flow;
So their Estates, that use it, come and go.*

OBSERVATION.

THE sea hath its alternate course and motion, its ebbings and flowings: no sooner is it high-water, but it begins to ebb again; and leave the shore naked and dry, which but a little before it covered and over-flowed. And as its tides so also its waves are the emblem of inconstancy, still rolling and tumbling, this way and that, never fixt and quiet. *Instabilis unda* : *As fickle as a wave*, is common to a Proverb. See James i. 6. *He that wavereth is like a wave of the sea, driven with winds, and tossed.* So Isai. lvii. 20. *It cannot rest.*

APPLICATION.

Thus mutable and inconstant are all outward things, there is no depending on them : nothing of any substance, or any solid consistence in them, 1 Cor. vii. 31. *The fashion of this world passeth away.* It is an high point of folly to depend upon such vanities, Prov. xxiii. 5. *Why wilt thou set* (or as it is in the *Hebrew*) *cause thine eyes to fly upon that which is not ? For riches certainly make themselves wings and fly away, as an eagle towards heaven.* In flying to us (saith *Augustine*) they have *alas vix quidem passerinas*, scarce a sparrow's wings ; but in flying from us, wings as an eagle. And those wings they are said to make to themselves, (*i. e.*) the cause of its transitoriness is in itself ; the creature is subjected to vanity by sin : They are sweet flowers, but withered presently, James i. 10. *As the flower of the grass, so shall the rich man fade away.* The man is like the stalk of the grass ; his riches are the flower of the grass ; his glory and outward beauty, the stalk is soon withered, but the flower much sooner. This is either withered upon, or blown off from it, while the stalk abides. Many a man

N

out lives his estate and honour, and stands in the world as a bare dry stalk in the field, whose flower, beauty, and bravery is gone; one puff of wind blows it away, one churlish easterly blast shrivels it up, 1 *Pet.* iv. 24.

How mad a thing is it then, for any man to be lifted up in pride, upon such a vanity as this is; to build so lofty and over-jetting roof upon such a feeble tottering foundation? We have seen meadows full of such curious flowers, mown down and withered, men of great estates impoverished suddenly: and when, like a meadow that is mown, they have begun to recover themselves again, (as the phrase is) the Lord hath sent *Grashoppers in the beginning of the shooting up of the latter growth,* Amos vii. 1. Just as the grashoppers and other creatures devour the second tender herbage, as soon as the field begins to recover its verdure. So men, after they have been denuded and blasted by providence, they begin after a while to flourish again, but then comes some new affliction, and blasts all. None have more frequent experience of this, than you that are merchants and sea-men, whose estates are floating: and yet such as have had the highest security in the eye of reason, have notwithstanding experienced the vanity of these things. *Henry* the fourth a potent prince, was reduced to such a low ebb, that he petitioned for a Prebend's place in the Church of *Spire*. *Gallimer*, king of the *Vandals*, was brought so low, that he sent to his friend for a spunge, a loaf of bread and an harp: a spunge to dry up his tears, a loaf of bread to maintain his life, and an harp to solace himself in his misery. The story of *Bellisarius* is very affecting: He was a man famous in his time, general of an army, yet having his eyes put out, and stripped of all earthly comforts, was led about, crying, *Date obolum* Bellisario, Give one penny to poor *Bellisarius*. Instances in history of this kind are infinite. Men of the greatest estates and honours, have nevertheless become the very *Ludibria fortunæ*, as one speaks, The very scorn of fortune.

Yea, and not only wicked men, that have gotten their estates by rapine and oppression, have lived to see them thus scattered by providence: but sometimes godly men have had their estates, how justly soever acquired, thus scattered by providence also. Who ever had an estate better gotten, better bottomed, or better managed, than *Job*? yet all was overthrown and swept away in a moment: though in mercy to him, as the issue demonstrated.

Oh then! what a vanity is it to set the heart and let out the affections on them! You can never depend too much upon God, nor too little upon the creature, 1 Tim. vi. 17. "Charge them that are rich in this world, that they be not high minded and trust in uncertain riches."

REFLECTION.

Are all earthly things thus transitory and vain? Then what a reproach and shame is it to me, that the men of this world should be more industrious and eager in the prosecution of such vanities, than I am to enrich my soul with solid and everlasting treasure? O that ever a sensual lust should be more operative in them than the love of God in me! O my soul, thou dost not lay out thy strength and earnestness for heaven, with any proportion to what they do for the world. I have indeed higher motives, and a surer reward than they: But as I have an advantage above them herein, so they have an advantage above me in the strength and intireness of the principle by which they are acted. What they do for the world, they do it with all their might; they have no contrary principle to oppose them; their thoughts, strength, and affections are intirely carried in one channel: But I find *a law in my members warring against the law of my mind*; I must strive through a thousand difficulties and contradictions, to the discharge of a duty. O my God! Shall not my heart be more enlarged in zeal, love, and delight in thee, than theirs are after their lusts? O let me once find it so.

Again, is the creature so vain and unstable, then why are my affections so hot and eager after it? And why am I so apt to dote upon its beauty, especially when God is staining all its pride and glory! *Jer.* xlv. 5, 6. Surely it is unbecoming the spirit of a Christian at any time; but at such a time we may say of it, as *Hushai* of *Abithophel*'s counsel, *It is not good at this time.*

O that my spirit were raised above them, and my conversation more in heaven! O that like that angel, *Rev.* x. 1, 2. which came down from heaven, and set one foot upon the sea, and another upon the earth, having a crown upon his head, so I might set one foot upon all the cares, fears, and terrors of the world, and another upon all the tempting splendour and glory of the world, treading both under foot in the dust, and crowning myself with nothing but spiritual excellencies and glory!

THE POEM.

Judge in thyself (O Christian) is it meet
To set thy heart on what beasts set their feet?

" 'Tis no *hyperbole*, if you be told,
" You dig for dross with mattocks made of gold,
" Affections are too costly to bestow
" Upon the fair-fac'd nothings here below.
" The eagle scorns to fall down from on high
" (The proverb saith) to catch the silly flie.
" And can a Christian leave the face of God,
" T' embrace the earth, or dote upon a clod?
" Can earthly things thy heart so strangely move,
" To tempt it down from the delights above;
" And now to court the world at such a time
" When God is laying judgment to the line?
" It's just like him that doth his cabin sweep
" And trim, when all is sinking in the deep;
" Or like the silly bird, that to her nest
" Doth carry straws, and never is at rest,
" Till it be feather'd well, but doth not see
" The ax beneath that's hewing down the tree.
" If on a thorn thy heart itself repose
" With such delight, what if it were a rose?
" Admire, O saint, the wisdom of thy God,
" Who of the self-same tree doth make a rod,
" Lest thou shouldst surfeit on forbidden fruit,
" And live not like a saint, but like a brute."

CHAP. XVIII.

Like hungry lions, waves for sinners gape:
Leave then your sins behind, if you'll escape.

OBSERVATION.

THE waves of the sea are sometimes raised by God's commission, to be executioners of his threatnings upon sinners: When *Jonah* fled from the presence of the Lord to *Tarshish*, the text saith, " The Lord sent out a great wind into the sea, and there was a mighty tempest, so that the ship was like to be broken," Jonah i. 4. These were God's bailiffs, to arrest the run-away prophet. And Psal. cxlviii. 8. The stormy winds are said to *fulfil his word*; not only his word of command, in rising when God bids them, but his word of *threatning* also. And hence it is called a *destroying wind*, Jer. li. 1. and a *stormy wind in God's fury*, Ezek. xiii. 13.

APPLICATION.

If these be the executioners of God's threatning, how sad then is their condition that put forth to sea under the guilt of all their sins? O, if God should commissionate the winds to go after and arrest thee for all thou owest him, where art thou then? How dare you put forth under the power of a divine threat, before all be cleared betwixt God and thee? Sins in Scripture are called debts, Mat. vi. 12. They are debts to God; not that we owe them to him, or ought to sin, but *metonymically*, because they render the sinner obnoxious to God's judgments, even as pecuniary debts oblige him that hath not wherewith to pay, to suffer punishment. All sinners must undergo the curse, either in their own person, according to the express letter of the law, Gen. ii. 17. Gal. iii. 10. or their surety, according to the tacit intent of the law, manifested to be the mind of the law-giver, Gen. iii. 15. Gal. iii. 13, 14.

Now he that by faith hath interest in this surety, hath his discharge, his *Quietus est*, sealed in the blood of Christ; all process at law, or from the law, is stopt. Rom. viii. 1. But if thou be an impenitent perſiſting ſinner, thy debt remains upon thine own ſcore. "And be ſure thy ſin will find thee out where ever thou goeſt," Num. xxxii. 23. *(i.e.)* God's revenging hand for ſin will be upon thee: Thou maiſt loſe the ſight and memory of thy ſins, but they loſe not the ſight of thee; they follow after, as the hound doth the fleeting game upon the ſcent, till they have fetcht thee up: And then conſider, "How fearful a thing it is to fall into the hands of the living God," Heb. x. 31. How ſoon may a ſtorm arreſt, and bring thee before the bar of God?

REFLECTION.

O my ſoul, what a caſe art thou in, if this be ſo? Are not all thy ſins yet upon thine own ſcore? Haſt not thou made light of Chriſt, and that precious blood of his, and hitherto perſiſted in thy rebellion againſt him? And what can the iſſue of this be at laſt, but ruin? There is abundant mercy indeed for returning ſinners; but the goſpel ſpeaks of none for perſiſting and impenitent ſinners. And though many who are going on in their ſins are overtaken by grace, yet there is no grace promiſed to ſuch as go on in ſin. O, if God ſhould arreſt me by the next ſtorm, and call me to an account for all that I owe him, I muſt then ly in the priſon of hell to all eternity; for I can never pay the debt; nay, all the angels in heaven cannot ſatisfy for it. Being Chriſtleſs, I am under all the curſes in the book of God; a child of *Hagar*. Lord, pity and ſpare me a little longer! O diſcover thy Chriſt unto me, and give me faith in his blood, and then thou art fully ſatisfied at once, and I diſcharged for ever. O require not the debt at my hand, for then, thou wilt never be ſatisfied, nor I acquitted. What profit, Lord, is there in my blood! O my soul, make haste to this Christ, thy refuge city; thou knowest not how soon the avenger of blood may overtake thee.

THE POEM.

' Thy sins are debts, God puts them to account;
' Canst tell, poor wretch, to what thy debts amount?
' Thou fill'st the treasure of thy sins each hour,
' Into his vials God doth also pour
' Proportionable wrath: Thou seest it not;
' But yet assure thyself, there's drop for drop.
' For every sand of patience running out,
' A drop of wrath runs in. Soul, look about.
' God's treasure's almost full, as well as thine:
' When both are full, O then the dreadful time
' Of reckoning comes; thou shalt not gain a day
' Of patience more, but then there hastes away
' Heaven's pursivant, who comes upon the wing
' With his commission seal'd, to take and bring.
' Do'st still reject Christ's tenders? Well, next storm
' May be the bailiff ordered to perform
' This dreadful office. O then restless be,
' Till God in Christ be reconcil'd to thee.
' The sum is great, but if a Christ thou get,
' Fear not, a Prince can pay a beggar's debt.
' Now if the storm should rise, thou need not fear;
' Thou art, but the delinquent is not there.
' A pardon'd soul to sea may boldly go:
' He fears not bailiffs, that doth nothing owe.''

CHAP. XIX.

To save the ship, rich ladings cast away,
Thy soul is shipwreck'd if thy lusts do stay.

OBSERVATION.

IN storms and distresses at sea, the richest commodities are cast over board; they stand not upon it, when life and all is in jeopardy and hazard. Jonah i. 5. *The mariners cast forth the wares that were in the ship into the sea, to lighten it.* And Acts xxvii. 18, 19. they cast out the very tacklings of the ship. How highly soever men prize such commodities, yet reason tells them, It were better these should perish, than life. Satan himself could say, Job i. *Skin for skin, and all that a man hath will he give for his life.*

APPLICATION.

And surely it is every way as highly reasonable, that men should mortify, cast out, and cut off their dearest lusts, rather than their immortal souls should sink and perish in the storm of God's wrath. Life indeed, is a precious treasure, and highly valued by men: You know what *Solomon* saith, Eccles. ix. 4. That *a living dog is better than a dead lion.* And we find men willing to part with their estates, limbs;

or any outward comfort, for the prefervation of it. The woman in the gofpel fpent all fhe had on the phyficians for her health, a degree below life. Some men indeed do much overvalue their lives, and part with Chrift and peace of confcience for it; but he that thus faves it, fhall loofe it. Now if life be fo much worth, what then is the foul worth? Alas! life is but a *vapour, which appeareth for a little while, and then vanifheth away*, James iv. 14.

Life indeed is more worth than all the world, but my foul is more worth than ten thoufand lives; Nature teacheth you to value the firft fo high, and grace fhould teach you to value the fecond much higher, Mat. xix. 26. Now here is the cafe: either you muft part with your fins, or with your fouls; if thefe be not caft out, both muft fink together. *If ye live after the flefh, ye muft die*, Rom. viii. 13. God faith to you in this cafe, as to *Abab*, when he fpared *Benhadad*, 1 Kings xx. 42. "Becaufe thou haft let go a man which God hath appointed to deftruction, therefore thy life fhall go for his life." Guilt will raife a ftorm of wrath, as *Jonah* did, if not caft out.

REFLECTION.

And muft fin or the foul perifh? Muft my life, yea, my eternal life go for it, if I fpare it? O then let me not be cruel to mine own foul, in fparing my fin; O my foul, this foolifh pity, and cruel indulgence will be thy ruin; If I fpare it, God hath faid, *He will not fpare me*, Deut. xxvi. 20. It is true, the pains of mortification are fharp, but yet it is eafier than the pains of hell. To cut off a right hand or pluck out a right eye, is hard; but to have my soul cut off eternally from God, is harder. Is it as easy (O my soul!) to burn for them in hell, as to mortify them on earth? Surely, it is "profitable for me, that one member perish, rather than that all be cast into hell," Mat. v. 24. I see the merchant willing to part with rich wares, if embarqued with them in a storm: And those that have gangreen'd legs or arms, willingly stretch them out to be cut off to preserve life: And shall I be willing to endure no difficulties for my soul? Christ reckoned souls worth his blood, And is it not worth my self-denial? Lord, let me not warm a snake in my bosom, that will at last sting me to the heart.

THE POEM.

' Thy soul's the ship, its lading is its lusts,
' God's judgments stormy winds and dang'rous gust,
' Conscience the master; but the stubborn will
' Goes *suprar cargo*, and doth keep the bill.
' Affections are the men the winds do rise,
' The storm increases: conscience gives advice,
' To throw those lusts o'er-board, and so to ease
' The vessel, which else cannot keep the Seas.
' The will opposes, and th' affections say,
' The master's counsel they will not obey.
' The case is dangerous, that no man can doubt,
' Who sees the storm within, and that without.
' Lusts and affections cannot part, no, rather,
' They are resolv'd to swim or sink together.
' Conscience still strives, but they cannot abide
' That it or reason should the case decide.

'Lust knows what reason in like cases still
'Determines well: Then chuse ye whom ye will,
'Shall's make the Devil judge? This case has been
'Before him, and he judg'd, that skin for skin,
'And all men have, they'll part with for their life.
'Then how unreasonable is this strife?
'They that their sins do with their persons ship,
'Do for their souls prepare a dreadful whip.

CHAP. XX.

Christ with a word can surging waves appease;
His voice a troubled soul can quickly ease.

OBSERVATION.

WHEN the sea works, and is tempestuous, it is not in the power of any creature to appease it. When the Egyptians would by their hieroglyphicks express an impossibility, they did it by the picture of a man treading upon the waves. It is storied of *Canute*, an ancient *Danish* King, That when a mighty storm of flattery arose upon him, he appeased it by shewing that he could not appease the sea: But one of his courtiers told him, as he rode near the sea-side, That he was lord of the sea, as well as land. Well, said the king, we shall see that by and by; and so went to the water-side, and with a loud voice cried, 'O ye seas and waves, come no further, touch not my feet.' But the sea came up, notwithstanding that charge, and confuted the flattery. But now Jesus Christ hath the command of them indeed: It is said of him, Mat. viii. 26. *That he rebuked them.* And Mark iv. 38. He quiets them with a word, *Peace, be still:* as one would hush a child, and it obeyed him.

APPLICATION.

Conscience, when awakened by the terrors of the Lord, is like a raging tempestuous sea; so it works, so it roars; and it is not in the power of all creatures to hush or quiet it. Spiritual terrors, as well as spiritual consolations, are not known till felt. O when the arrows of the Almighty are shot into the spirit, and the terrors of God set themselves in array against the soul; when the venom of those arrows drink up the spirits, and those armies of terrors charge violently and successively upon it, as Job vi. 4. What creature then is able to stand before them! Even God's own dear children have felt such terrors, as have *distracted them,* Psal. lxxxi. 15. Conscience is the seat of guilt. It is like a burning glass, so it contracts the beams of the threatnings, twists them together, and reflects them on the soul, until it smoke, scorch, and flame. If the wrath of a king be like the roaring of a lion, then what is the Almighty's wrath! which is *burning wrath,* Job xix. 11. *Tearing wrath,* Psal. l. 22. *Surprizing wrath,* Job xx. 23. And *Abiding wrath,* Job iii. 36.

In this case no creature can relieve, all are physicians of no value; some under these terrors, have thought hell more tolerable, and by a violent hand have thrust themselves out of the world into it, to avoid these gnawings; Yet Jesus Christ can quickly calm these mystical waves also, and hush them with a word; yea he is the Physician, and no other. It is the sprinkling of his blood, which, like a cooling fomentation, allays those heats within; That blood of sprinkling speaks peace, when all others have practised upon the soul to no purpose; and the reason is, because he is a person in whom God and man, justice and mercy meet, and kiss each other, Eph. ii. 14. And hence faith fetches in peace to the soul, Rom. v. 1.

REFLECTION.

Can none appease a troubled conscience, but Christ? Then learn, O my soul, to understand and daily more and more to favour that glorious name, even Jesus, that delivers not only from the wrath to come, but that which is felt here also. Oh if the foretaste of hell be so intolerable, if a few drops let fall on the conscience in this life, be so scalding and insufferable; what is it to have all the vials poured out to eternity, when there shall be nothing to divert, mitigate, or allay it?

Here men have somewhat to abate those terrors, some hopes of mercy, at least a possibility; but there, there is none. O my soul! how art thou loaded with guilt! and what a *Magormissabib* wouldst thou be, should God rouze that sleepy lion in thy bosom! My condition is not at all the better, because my conscience is quiet. Ah, the day is coming, when it must awake, and will lighten and thunder terribly within me, if I get not into Christ the sooner. O Lord, who knows the power of thy wrath? O let me not carry this guilt out of the world with me, to maintain those everlasting flames? let me give no sleep to mine eyes, nor slumber to my eye-lids, till I feel the comfort of that blood of sprinkling, which alone speaketh peace.

THE POEM.

' Among the dreadful works of God, I find
' No *metaphors*, to paint a troubled mind.
' I think on this, now that, and yet will neither
' Come fully up, though all be put together.
' 'Tis like the raging sea, that casts up mire,
' Or like to *Etna*, breathing smoke and fire;
' Or like a rouzed lion fierce and fell;
' Or like those furies that do howl in hell.
' O conscience! Who can stand before thy power,
' Endure thy gripes and twinges but an hour?
' Stone, gout, strapado, racks, whatever is
' Dreadful to sense, is but a toy to this.
' No pleasures, riches, honours, friends can tell
' How to give ease: in this 'tis like to hell.
' Call for the pleasant timbrel, lute, and harp;
' Alas! the musick howls; the pain's too sharp
' For these to charm, divert or lull asleep:
' These cannot reach it; no, the wound's too deep.
' Let all the promises before him stand,
' And set a *Barnabas* at its right-hand;
' These in themselves no comfort can afford,
' 'Tis Christ, & none but Christ, can speak the word.
' And he no sooner speaks, but all is calm,
' The storm is over, and the mind tranquil;

'There goes a Power with his majestick voice,
'To hush the dreadful storm, and still its noise.
'Who would not fear and love this glorious Lord,
'That can rebuke such tempests with a word?

CHAP. XXI.

Our food out of the Sea God doth command;
Yet few therein take notice of his hand.

OBSERVATION.

THE providence of God in furnishing us with such plenty and variety of fish, is not slightly to be past over. We have not only several sorts of fish in our own seas, which are caught in their seasons; but from several parts, especially the western parts of *England*, many sail of ships are sent yearly to the *American* parts of the world; as *New-foundland*, *New-England*, &c. Whence every year is brought home, not only enough to supply our own nation, but many thousand pounds worth also yearly returned from *Spain*, and other countries; by which trade many thousand families do subsist.

APPLICATION.

But, now, what returns do we make to heaven for these mercies? O what notice is taken of the good hand of providence, which thus supplies and feeds us with the bleſſings of the ſea ? I fear there are but few that own, or act in ſubmiſſion to it, and are careful to return according to received benefit. Men do not conſider, " That their works are in the hand of God," Eccleſ. ix. 1. And even thoſe that have the moſt immediate dependence upon providence, as merchants and ſeamen, yet are very prone to undertake deſigns in the confidence of their own wiſdom and induſtry; not looking higher for the bleſſing, James iv. 13. They often " ſacrifice to their own net, and burn incenſe to their drag, becauſe by them their portion is fat and their meat plenteous," Hab. i. 16. *viz.* They attribute what is due to God, unto the creature. Now this is a ſin highly provoking to the Lord: for look in what degree the heart cleaves to the ſecond cauſe, in the ſame degree it departs from the living God, Jer. x. 5.

And how do you think the bleſſed God will take it, to ſee himſelf thus debaſed, and the creature thus exalted into his place, to ſee you carry yourſelves to the creature as to a God, and to the bleſſed God, as to a creature. Surely, it is a great and common evil and ſuch as will blaſt all, if not timely diſcovered and lamented. If we make fleſh our arm, it's juſt with God to wither and dry up that arm. Do we not, my brethren, look upon ſecond cauſes, as if they had the main ſtroke in our buſineſs ? And with a neglective eye paſs by God, as as if he came in but collaterally, and on the by, into it ? But certainly, all endeavours will be unſanctified, if not ſucceſsleſs, in which God is not eyed and engaged.

" It is in vain for you to riſe up early, and ſit up late, and eat the bread of ſorrows ; for ſo he giveth his beloved sleep," Psal. cxxvii. 2. *(i. e.)* It is to no purpose for men to beat their brains, tire their spirits, and crack their consciences for an estate. The true way of acquiring and enjoying the creature, is by submitting quietly to the will of God, in a prudent and diligent, yet moderate use of lawful means: Nothing can thrive with us till then.

REFLECTION.

Why then should I disquiet myself in vain; and rob myself of my peace, by these unbelieving cares and distractions? O this hath been my sin! I have acted, as if my condition had been at my own dispose; I have eyed creatures and means too much, and God too little. How have my hands hanged down with discouragement, when second causes have disappeared, or wrought cross to my designs in the world, ready to transfer the fault on this thing, or that! and again, how apt am I to be vainly lifted up in carnal confidence, when I see myself competently furnished with creature munition and provision? Oh, what a God-provoking wickedness is this! How oft hath providence checked my carnal presumption, and dashed many hopeful projects? yet have I not owned it, as I ought, and submitted to it. Oh, it is a wonder this hath not closed the hand of Providence against me, and pulled down a curse upon all! Ah Lord, let me now learn to " acquaint myself with thee, then shall I decree a thing, and it shall be established," Job xx. 28.

THE POEM.

' In all the gifts of God we should advance
' His glorious name; not say, it came by chance.
' Or to the idol of our prudence pay
' The tribute of his praise, and go our way.
' The waves do clap their hands, and in their kind
' Acknowledge God; and what, are they more blind
' That float upon them? yea, for what they get,
' They offer sacrifices to their net.
' This is your manner, thus to work you go:
' Confess the naked truth; say, is't not so?
' This net was wisely cast, 'tis full, 'tis full:
' O well done mates, this is a gallant pull.
' Thus what is due to God, you do apply
' Unto yourselves most sacrilegiously.
' I cannot wonder such come empty home,
' That are so full of self and sin: yet some
' I hope look higher, and on God reflect
' Due praise. A blessing such may well expect."

CHAP. XXII.

*Whilst thou by art the silly fish dost kill,
Perchance the Devil's hook sticks in thy gill.*

OBSERVATION.

THERE is skill in fishing; they that go to sea in a fishing voyage, use to go provided with their craft (as they very fitly call it) without which they can do nothing. They have their lines, hooks of several sizes, and their bait: They carefully observe their seasons; when the fish falls in, then they ply their business day and night.

APPLICATION.

But how much more skilful and industrious is Satan to ensnare and destroy souls? The devil makes a voyage as well as you; he hath his baits for you, as you for the fish: he hath his devices and wiles to catch souls, 2 Cor. ii. 11. Ephes. vi. 11. He is a serpant, an old serpant, Rev. xii. 9. Too crafty for man in his perfection, much more in his collapsed and degenerated state, his understanding being cracked by the fall, and all his faculties poisoned and perverted.

Divines observe four steps, or degrees of Satan's tempting power.

First, He can find out the constitution-evils of men; he knows to what sin their natures are more especially prone and inclinable.

Secondly, He can propound suitable objects to those lusts, he can exactly and fully hit every mans humour. As *Agrippina* mixed her poison in that meat her husband loved best.

Thirdly, He can inject and cast motions into the mind, to close with those tempting objects; as it is said of *Judas*, John xiii. 2. "The devil put it into his heart."

Fourthly, He can sollicite, irritate, and provoke the heart, and by those continual restless solicitations weary it; and hereby he often draws men to commit such things as startled them in the first motion.

All this can he do, if he find the work stick, and meet with rubs and difficulties; yet doth he not act to the utmost of his skill and power, at all times and with all persons; neither indeed need he so to do, the very propounding of an object, is enough to some, without any further sollicitation: The devil makes an easy conquest of them.

And beside all this, his policy much appears in the election of place, time and instruments to tempt by: And thus are poor souls caught, as fishes in an evil net, Eccles. ix. 12. The carnal man is led by sense, as the beast; and satan handles and fits him accordingly. He useth all sorts of motives, not only internal, and intellective, but external and sensitive also; as the sparkling of the wine, when it gives its colour in the glass: the harlot's beauty, whose eye-lids are snares; hiding always the hook, and concealing the issue from them. He promises them gain and profit, pleasure and delight, and all that is tempting, with assurance of secresy. By these he fastens the fatal hook in their jaws, and thus they are led captive by him at his will.

REFLECTION.

And is satan so subtle and industrious to entice souls to sin? doth he thus cast out his golden baits, and allure souls with pleasure to their ruin? Then how doth it behove thee, O my soul, to be jealous and wary! How strict a guard should I set upon every sense! Ah, let me not so much regard how sin comes towards me in the temptation, as how it goes off at laſt. The day in which *Sodom* was deſtroyed, began with a pleaſant Sun-ſhine, but ended in fire and brimſtone. I may promiſe myſelf much content in the ſatisfaction of my luſts: But O, how certainly will it end in my ruin! *Ahab* doubtleſs promiſed himſelf much content in the vineyard of *Naboth*, but his blood paid for it in the portion of *Jezreel*. The harlot's bed was perfumed to entice the ſimple young man, Prov. vii. 17. But thoſe chambers of delight proved the chambers of death, and her houſe the way to hell. Ah, with what a ſmiling face doth ſin come on towards me in its temptations! how doth it tickle the carnal fancy, and pleaſe the deceived heart? But what a dreadful cataſtrophe and upſhot hath it? The delight is quickly gone, but the guilt thereof remains to amaze and terrify the ſoul with ghaſtly forms, and dreadful repreſentations of the wrath of God: As ſin hath its delights attending it to enter and faſten it, ſo it hath its horrors and ſtings to torment and wound: And as certainly as I ſee thoſe go before it to make away, ſo certainly ſhall I find theſe follow after, and tread upon its heels. No ſooner is the conſcience awakened, but all thoſe delights vaniſh as a night-viſion, or as a dream when one awakes; and then I ſhall cry, here is the hook, but where is the bait? Here is the guilt and horror, but where the delight that I was promiſed! And I, whither ſhall I now go? Ah my deceitful luſts! You have enticed and left me in the midſt of all miſeries,

THE POEM.

" There's skill in fishing, that the devil knows;
" For when for souls Satan a fishing goes,
" He angels cunningly: He knows he must
" Exactly fit the bait unto the lust.
" He studies constitution, place, and time,
" He guesses what is his delight, what thine;
" And so accordingly prepares the bait;
" Whilst he himself lies closely hid to wait
" When thou wilt nibble at it. Dost incline
" To drunken meetings? then he baits with wine,
" Is this his way; if unto this he'll smell,
" He'll shortly pledge a cup of wrath in hell.
" To pride or lust is thy nature bent?
" An object suitable he will present.
" O think on this, when you cast in the hook,
" Say, Thus for my poor soul doth Satan look.
" O play not with temptations; do not swallow
" The sugar'd bait, consider what will follow.
" If once he hitch thee, then away he draws
" Thy captive soul close prisoner in his paws.

CHAP. XXIII.

Doth trading fail, and voyages prove bad?
If you cannot discern the cause, 'tis sad.

OBSERVATION.

THERE are many sad complaints abroad (and I think not without cause) that trade fails, nothing turns to account. And though all countries be open, and free for traffick, and a general peace with all nations, yet there seems to be a dearth, a secret curse upon trading. You run from country to country, and come losers home. Men can hardly render a reason for it; few hit the right cause of this judgment.

APPLICATION.

That prosperity and success in trade is from the blessing of God, I suppose few are so atheistical, as once to deny or question. The devil himself acknowledges it, Job i. 10. "Thou hast blessed the work of his hands, and his substance is increased in the land." It is not in the power of any man to get riches, Deut. viii. 18. "Thou shalt remember the Lord thy God, for it is he that giveth thee power to get wealth." It is his blessing that makes good men rich, and his permission that makes wicked men rich. That maxim came from hell, *Quisque fortunæ suæ faber:* Every man is the contriver of his own condition: certainly, "The good of man is not in his own hand," Job xxi. 16. "Promotion cometh not from the east or west," Psal. lxxv. 6.

This being acknowledged, it is evident, that in all disappointment, and want of success in our callings, we ought not to stick in second causes, but to look higher, even to the hand and dispose of God: For, whose it is to give the blessing, his also it is to withhold it. And this is as clear in scripture as the other. It is the Lord that takes away the fishes of the sea, Hof. iv. 3. Zeph. i. 3. It is he that *curseth our blessings*, Mal. ii. 2.

This God doth as a punishment for sin, and the abuse for mercies: And therefore in such cases, we ought not to rest in general complaints to, or of one another, but search what those sins are that provoke the Lord to inflict such judgments.

And here I must request your patience, to bear a plain and close word of conviction. My brethren, I am persuaded these are the sins, among many others, that provoke the Lord to blast all your imployments.

1. Our undertaking designs without prayer. Alas, how few of us begin with God? Interest him in our dealings, and ask counsel and direction at his mouth. Prayer is that which sanctifies all employments and enjoyments, 1 Tim. iv. 5. The very heathen could say, *A Jove principium.* They must begin with God. O that we had more prayers and fewer oaths.

2. Injustice and fraud in our dealings. A sin to which merchants are prone, as appears by that expression, Hos. xii. 7. This is that which will blast all our enjoyments.

3. An over-earnest endeavour after the world. Men make this their business, they will be rich: And hence it is, they are not only unmerciful to themselves, in wearying and wasting their own spirits with carking cares, but to such also as they employ; neither regarding the souls or bodies of men: scarce affording them the liberty of the Lord's day (as hath been too common in our *New-found-Land* employments;) or if they have it, yet they are so worn out with incessant labours, that that precious time is spent either in sleep or idleness. It is no wonder God gives you more rest than you would have, since that day of rest hath been no better improved. This over-doing hath not been the least cause of our undoing.

Lastly, Our abuse of prosperity, when God gave it; making God's mercies the food and fewel of our lusts. When we have an affluence and confluence of outward blessings, this made us *kick against God*, as Deut xxxiii. 15. *Forget God*, Deut. iv. 14. Yea, grow proud of our strength and riches, Ezek. xvi. 13. and Jer. ii. 31. Ah! How few of us in the days of our prosperity, behaved ourselves as good *Jehosaphat* did? 2 Chron. xvii. 5, 6. " He had silver and gold in abundance, and his heart was lifted in the way of God's commandments; not in pride and insolence.

REFLECTION.

Are these the sins that blast our blessings, and wither our mercies! O then let me cease to wonder it is no better, and rather admire that it is no worse with me; that my neglect of prayer, injustice in dealings, earthly-mindedness, and abuse of former mercies, have not provoked God to strip me naked of all my enjoyments. Let me humbly accept from the Lord the punishment of my iniquities, and lay my hand upon my mouth. And O that these disappointments might convince me of the creatures vanity, and cause me to drive on another trade for heaven; then shall I adore thy wisdom in rending from me those idolized enjoyments. Ah, Lord, when I had them, my heart was a perpetual drudge to them. How did I then forget God, neglect my duty and not mind my eternal concernments! Oh, if these had not perished, in all probability I had perished. My God, let my soul prosper, and then a small portion of these things shall afford me more comfort than ever I had in their greatest abundance. "A little that a righteous man hath, is better than the riches of many wicked," Psal. xxxvii. 16.

THE POEM.

"There's great complaint abroad that trading's bad
"You shake your head, and cry, 'Tis sad, 'tis sad.
"Merchants lay out their stock, seamen their pains,
"And in their eye they both may put their gains.
"Your fishing fails, you wonder why 'tis so,
"'Tis this (saith one) or that: but I say no;
"'Twill ne'er be well till, you confess and say,
"It is our sin that frights the fish away.
"No wonder all goes into bags with holes,
"Since so the gospel hath been in your souls.
"We kick'd, like *Jesurun*, when the flowing tide
"Of wealth came tumbling in, this nourish'd pride
"'Twixt soul and body, now I wish it may
"Fare as betwixt the *Jews* and us this day.
"O that our outward want and loss may be
"To us a soul enriching poverty!
"If disappointments here, advance the trade
"For heaven, then complain not; you have made
"The richest voyage, and your empty ships
"Return deep laden with soul benefits."

CHAP. XXIV.

In seas the greater fish the less devour:
So some men crush all those within their power.

OBSERVATION.

THERE are fishes of prey in the sea, as well as birds and beasts of prey on the land. Our seamen tell us, how the devouring whales, sharks, dolphins, and other fishes follow the caplein, and other smaller fish, and devour multitudes of them. It is frequent with us, in our own seas, to find several smaller fishes in the bellies of the greater ones; yea, I have often heard seamen say, That the poor little fry, when pursued, are so sensible of the danger, that they have sometimes seen multitudes of them cast themselves upon the shoar, and perish there, to avoid the danger of being devoured by them.

APPLICATION.

Thus cruel, merciless, and oppressive are wicked men, whose *tender mercies are cruelty*, Prov. xxii. 10. We see the like cruelty in our extortioners, and over reaching sharks ashore, who grind the faces of the poor, and regard not the cries of the fatherless and widows, but fill their houses with the gain of oppression. These are, by the holy Ghost, compared to the fishes of the sea, Hab. i. 13, 14. This is a crying sin, yea, it sends up a loud cry to heaven for vengeance, Exod. xxii. 23. "If thou afflict the widow and the fatherless, and they cry unto me, I will surely hear their cry." And verse 27. "I will hear his cry, for I am gracious. Nay, God will not only hear their cry, but avenge their quarrel. That is a remarkable text, 1 Thes. iv. 6. "That no man go beyond and defraud his brother in any matter, because that the Lord is the *Ecdicos.* (Avenger) of all such," This word is but once more used in the *New-Testament*, Rom. xiii. 4. And there it is applied to the civil magistrate, who is to see execution done upon offenders. But now this is a sin that sometimes may be out of the reach of man's justice, & therefore God himself will be their Avenger. You may overpower the poor in this world, and it may be they cannot contend with you at man's bar, therefore God will bring it before his bar.

Believe it, sirs, it is a sin so provoking to God, that he will not let it escape without severe punishment, sooner or later. The prophet *Habakkuk*, Chap. i. verse 13. wondered how the holy God could forbear such till the general day of reckoning and that he did not take exemplary vengeance on them in this life. "Thou art of purer eyes than to behold evil, and canst not look upon iniquity: Wherefore then lookest thou upon them that deal treacherously, and holdest thy tongue when the wicked devours the man that is more righteous than he?" And Prov. xxiii. 10, 11. "Enter not into the fields of the fatherless, *i. e.*" Of the poor and helpless. But why is it more dangerous violently to invade their right, than anothers? The reason is added, "For their Redeemer is mighty, and he shall plead their cause with thee." It may be they are not able to obtain a council to plead their cause here; therefore God will plead their cause for them.

REFLECTION.

Turn in upon thyself (O my soul) and consider, hast thou not been guilty of this crying sin? Have I not (when a servant) over-reached and defrauded others, and filled my master's house with violence and deceit? and so brought myself under that dreadful threatening, Zeph. i, 9. Or since I came to trade and deal upon my own account, have not the ballances of deceit been in my hand? I have (it may be) kept many in my service and employment; have not I used their labours without reward, and so am under that woe? Jer. xxii. 13. Or not given them wages proportionable to their work? Isai. lviii. 3. Or by pad payment and unjust deductions and allowances defrauded them of a part of their due? Mal. iii. 5. Or at least delayed payment, out of a covetous disposition to gain by it; whilst their necessities in the mean time cryed aloud for it; and so sinned against God's express commands, Deut. xxiv. 14, 15. Levit. xix. 30. Or have I not persecuted such as God hath smitten? Psal. lxix. 26. And rigorously exacted the utmost of my due, though the hand of God hath gone out against them, breaking their estates? O my soul, examine thyself upon these particulars; rest not quiet, until this guilt be removed by the application of the blood of sprikling. Hath not the Lord said, James ii. 13. "That they shall have judgment without mercy, that hath shewed no mercy? And is it not a fearful thing to fall into the hands of the living God, *who hath said,* He will take vengeance for these things?

THE POEM.

" Devouring whales and ravenous sharks do follow
" The lesser fry, and at one gulp do swallow
" Some hundreds of them, as our seamen say;
" But we can tell far stranger things than they.
" For we have sharks ashore, on every creek,
" That to devour poor men do hunt and seek.
" No pity, sense, or bowels in them be,
" Nay, have they not put off humanity?
" Extortioners and cheaters, whom God hates,
" Have dreadful open mouths, and through those gates
" Brave persons with their heritages pass
" In funeral state, friends crying out alas!
" O give me *Agur's* wish, that I may never
" Be such myself, or feel the hands of either.
" And as for those that in their paws are grip'd,
" Pity and rescue, Lord, from that sad plight.
" When I behold the squeaking lark, that's born
" In falcon's talons, crying, bleeding, torn;
" I pity it's sad case, and would relieve
" The prisoner, if I could, as well as grieve.
" Fountain of pity, hear the piteous moans
" Of all thy captive and oppressed ones."

CHAP. XXV.

In storms to spread much sail endangers all :
So carnal mirth, if God for mourning call.

OBSERVATION.

IN storms at sea, the wise navigator will not spread much sail; that is the way to lose masts and all; They use then to furl up the sails, and lie a hull, when not able to bear a knot of sail; or else to lie a try, or scud before the wind and seas. It is no time then to hoist up the top and top-gallant, and shew their bravery.

APPLICATION.

When the judgments of God are abroad in the earth, it is no time then to make mirth, Ezek, xxi. 10. "should we (then) make mirth? It contemneth the rod of my son as every tree." (*i. e.*) As if it were a common rod, and ordinary affliction; whereas the rod of my son is not such as may be had of every tree; but it is an iron rod to such as despise it, Psal. ii. 9. O it is a provoking evil, and commonly God severely punishes it. Of all persons, such speed worst in the common calamity, Amos vi. 1. "Wo to them that are at ease in Sion, that are not grieved for the afflictions of *Joseph*," as verse 4. It may be (as one observes upon the text) they did not laugh at him, or break jests upon him; but they did not condole with him. And what shall be their punishment? See verse 7. "Therefore now shall they go captive with the first that go captive:" God will begin with them first. *Solomon* tells us, Eccles. iii. 4. "There is a time to weep, and a time to laugh; a time to mourn, and a time to dance:" Only *(as Master* Trap *notes upon the text)* "we must not invert the order, but weep with men, that we may laugh with angels." To be merry and frolicksome in a day of tribulation, is to disturb the order of seasons. That is a terrible text, Isa. xxii. 12. which should make the hearts of such as are guilty in this kind to tremble: "In that day did the Lord of hosts call to mourning, and to girding with sackcloth; and behold, joy and gladness; slaying oxen, killing sheep, drinking wine, &c." Well, what is the issue of this? Surely, this iniquity shall not be purged from you, till ye die. O dreadful word! Surely (my brethren) sympathy is a debt we owe to Christ mystical. Whatever our constitution, condition, or personal immunities be, yet when God calls for mourning, we must hear and obey that call. *David* was a king, an expert musician; a man of sanguine and chearful constitution; yet who more sensible of the evil of those times, than he? Rivers of water ran down his eyes at the consideration of them. *Melancthon* was so affected with the miseries of the church in his days, that he seemed to take little or no notice of the death of his child; whom he entirely loved. At such a time we may "say of laughter, Thou art mad, and of mirth, what doth it?"

REFLECTION.

Blush then, O my soul! for thy levity and insensibility under God's angry dispensations. How many of the precious sons and daughters of *Sion*, lie in tears abroad, while I have been " Nourishing my heart, as in a day of slaughter? The voice of God hath cried to the city, and men of understanding have heard its voice," Mic. vi. 9. But I have been deaf to that cry. How loth (my God) have I been to urge my sensual heart to acts of sorrow and mourning! Thou hast bid me weep with them that weep, but my vain heart cannot comply with such commands. Ah Lord! if I mourn not with *Sion*, neither shall I rejoice with her.

O, were mine eyes opened, and my heart sensible and tender, I might see cause enough to melt into tears; and like that christian *Niobe*, Luke vii. 38, to lie weeping at the feet of Christ. Lord, what stupidity is this? Shall I laugh when thou art angry, and thy children weeping and trembling? Then I may justly fear, lest " when they shall sing for joy of heart, I shall howl for vexation of spirit," Isai. lxv. 13, 14. Surely, O my soul! such laughter will be turned into mourning, either here or hereafter.

THE POEM.

" In troublous times mirth in the sinner's face
" Is like to a morning-cloak with silver lace.
" The lion's roaring makes the beasts to quake;
" God's roaring judgments cannot make us shake.
" What belluine contempt is this of God,
" To laugh in's face, when he takes up the rod?
" Such laughter God in tears will surely drown,
" (Unless he hate thee) e're he lay it down.

"These rods have voices; if thou hear them well:
"If not another rod's prepar'd in hell.
"And when the arm of God shall lay it on,
"Laugh if thou canst; no, then thy mirth is gone.
"All *Sion*'s children will lament and cry,
"When all her beauteous stones in dust do lie;
"And he that for her then laments and mourns,
"Shall want no joy, when God to her returns."

CHAP. XXVI.

A little leak neglected, dangerous proves;
One sin connived at, the soul undoes.

OBSERVATION.

THE smallest leak, if not timely discovered and stopt, is enough to sink a ship of the greatest burden; therefore seamen are wont frequently to try what water is in the hole; and if they find it fresh, and increasing upon them, they ply the pump, and presently set the carpenters to search for it and stop it; and till it be found they cannot be quiet.

APPLICATION.

What such a leak is to a ship, that is the smallest sin neglected to the soul; it is enough to ruin it eternally. For as the greatest sin, discovered, lamented, and mourned over by a believer, cannot ruin him; so the least sin indulged, covered, and connived at, will certainly prove the destruction of the sinner. No sin, though never so small, is tolerated by the pure and perfect law of God, Psalm cxix. 96. The *command is exceeding broad*; not as if it gave men a latitude to walk as they please, but *broad*, *i. e.* extending itself to all our words, thoughts, actions, and affections: Laying a law upon them all; conniving at no evil in any man, 1 Pet. ii. 1.

And as the word gives no allowance for the least sin, so it is the very nature of sincerity and uprightness, to set the heart against *(every)* way of wickedness, Psal. cxxxix. 23, 24. Job xxxi. 13. And especially against that sin which was its darling in the days of his vanity, Psalm xviii. 23. True hatred (as the philosopher observes) is of the whole † kind: He that hates sin as sin (and so doth every upright soul) hates all sins as well as some.

† *Eis ta gen.*

Again, the soul that hath had a saving sight of Jesus Christ, and a true discovery of the evil of sin, in the glass both of the law and gospel, can account no sin small. He knows the demerit of the smallest sin is God's eternal wrath, and that not the least sin can be remitted, without the shedding and application of the blood of Christ, Heb. ix. 22. which blood is of infinite value and price, 1 Pet. i. 19.

To conclude, God's people know, that little as well as great sins are dangerous, deadly and destructive in their own nature: A little poison will destroy a man. *Adrian* was choaked with a gnat; *Cæsar* stabbed with bodkins. A man would think *Adam*'s sin had been no great matter, yet what dreadful work did it make! It was not a single bullet to kill himself only; but as a chain-shot, which cut off all his poor miserable posterity. Indeed, no sin can be little, because its object against whom it is committed is so great, whence it receives a kind of infiniteneſs in itſelf, and becauſe the price paid to redeem us from it is ſo invaluable.

REFLECTION.

And is the ſmalleſt ſin not only damning in its own nature, but will certainly prove the ruin of that ſoul that hides and covers it? Oh then let my ſpirit accompliſh a diligent ſearch. Look to it, O my ſoul! that no ſin be indulged by thee. Set theſe conſiderations as ſo many flaming ſwords in the way of thy carnal delights and luſts: Let me never ſay of any ſin, as *Lot* did of *Zoar*, *it is a little one, ſpare it*. Shall I ſpare that which coſt the blood of Jeſus Chriſt? The Lord would not ſpare him, *when he made his ſoul an offering for ſin*, Rom. viii. 32. Neither will he ſpare me, if I defend and hide it, Deut. xxix. 20. Ah! If my heart were right, and my converſation ſound, that luſt, whatever it be, that is ſo favoured by me, would eſpecially be abhored and hated, Iſa. ii. 20. and xxx. 22. Whatever my convictions and reformations have been, yet if there be but one ſin retained and delighted in, this keeps the devil's intereſt ſtill in my ſoul: and though for a time he ſeem to depart, yet at laſt he will return with ſeven worſe ſpirits, and this is the ſin that will open the door to him, and deliver up my ſoul, Mat. xii. 43, 44. Lord, let me make thorough work of it: let me cut it off, and pluck it out, though it be as a right hand, or eye. Ah, ſhall I come ſo near the kingdom of God, and make ſuch a fair offer for Chriſt, and yet ſtick at a ſmall matter, and loſe all for want of one thing? Lord, let me ſhed the blood of the deareſt luſt, for his ſake that ſhed his deareſt blood for me.

THE POEM.

' There's many a soul eternally undone
' For sparing sin, because a little one.
' But we are much deceiv'd; no sin is small,
' That wounds so great a God, so dear a soul.
' Yet say it were, the smallest pen-knife may
' As well as sword or lance dispatch and slay.
' And shall so small a matter part and sever
' Christ and thy soul? What, make you part for ever?
' Or wilt thou stand on toys with him, when he
' Deny'd himself in greatest things for thee?
' Or will it be an ease in hell, to think
' How easily thy soul therein did sink?
' Are Christ and hell for trifles sold and bought?
' Strike souls with trembling, Lord, at such a thought!
' By little sins, belov'd, the soul is lost,
' Unless such sins, do great repentance cost.''

CHAP. XXVII.

*Ships make much way when they a trade-wind get,
With such a wind the saints have ever met.*

OBSERVATION.

THOUGH in most parts of the world the winds are variable, and sometimes blow from every point of the compass, by reason whereof, sailing is slow, and dangerous; yet about the Equinoctial, seamen meet with a trade-wind, blowing, for the most part, one way; and there they sail jocund before it, and scarce need to lower a top-sail for some hundreds of leagues.

APPLICATION.

Although the people of God meet with many seeming rubs and set-backs in their way to heaven, which are like contrary winds to a ship; yet are they from the day of their conversion, to the day of their complete salvation, never out of a trade-wind's way to heaven. Rom. viii. 21. " We know that all things work together for good, to them that love God, to them that are called according to his purpose." This is a most precious scripture, pregnant with its consolation to all believers in all conditions, a pillar of comfort to all distressed saints: Let us look a little nearer to it.

(We know) Mark the certainty and evidence of the proposition, which is not built upon a guess or remote probability, but upon the knowledge of the saints; *we know it*, and that partly by divine revelation, God has told us so; and partly by our own experience, we find it so.

(That all things). Not only things that lie in a natural and direct tendency to our good; as *ordinances, promises, blessings, &c.* but even such things as have no natural fitness and tendency to such an end; as *afflictions, temptations, corruptions, desertions, &c.* all these help onward. They

(Work together.) Not all of them directly, and of their own nature and inclination; but by being over-ruled and determined to such an issue by the

gracious hand of God: Nor yet do they work out such good to the saints, singly, and apart, but as adjuvant causes or helps, standing under, and working in subordination to the supreme and principal cause of their happiness.

Now, the most seeming opposite things, yea, sin in itself, which in its own nature is really opposite to their good, yet eventually contributes to it. Afflictions and desertions seem to work against us, but being once put into the rank and order of causes, they work together with such blessed instruments, as word and prayer, to an happy issue. And though the faces of these things, that so agree and work together, look contrary ways; yet there are, as it were, secret chains and connexions of providence betwixt them, to unite them in their issue. There may be many instruments employed about one work, and yet not communicate counsels, or hold intelligence with each other. *Joseph's* brethren, the *Midianites*, *Potiphar*, &c. knew not one another's mind; nor aimed at one end, (much less the end that God brought about by them) one acts out of revenge, another for gain, a third out of policy; yet all meet together at last, in that issue God had designed to bring about by them, even *Joseph's* advancement. Even so it is here, christian, there are more instruments at work for thine eternal good, than thou art aware of.

REFLECTION.

Chear up then, O my soul, and lean upon this pillar of comfort in all distresses. Here is a promise for me, if I am a called one; that like the philosopher's stone, turns all into gold it toucheth: This promise is my security; however things go in the world, my God "will do me no hurt," Jer. xxv. 6. Nay, he will do me good by every dispensation. "O that I had but an heart to make all things work for his glory, that thus causeth every thing to work for my good." My God, dost thou turn every thing to my advantage? O let me return all to thy praise; and if by every thing thou work my eternal good, then let me in every thing give thanks.

But ah! how foolish and ignorant have I been? even as a beast before thee. How hath my heart been disquieted, and apt to repine at thy dispensations, when they have crossed my will? not considering that my God faithfully pursues my good, even in those things that cross, as well as in that which pleases me.

Blessed Lord! what a blessed condition are all thy people in, who are within the line of this promise? All things friendly and beneficial to them; friends helpful; enemies helpful; every thing conspiring, and conducing to their happiness. With others it is not so; nothing works for their good; nay, every thing works against it: their very mercies are snares, and their prosperity destroys them; Prov. i. 32. even the blessed gospel itself is a favour of death to them: when evil befals them, "it is an only evil," Ezek. vii. 5. that is, not turned into good to them; and as their evils are not turned into good, so all their good is turned into evil. As this promise hath an influence into all that concerns the people of God, so the curse hath an influence into all the enjoyments of the wicked. O my soul, bless the Lord, who hath cast thy lot into such a pleasant place, and given thee such a glorious heritage, as this promise is.

S

THE POEM.

"When once the dog-star rises, many say,
"Corn ripens then apace, both night and day.
"Souls once in Christ, that morning-star lets fall
"Such influences on them, that all
"God's dispensations to them then, sweet or sour,
"Ripen their souls for glory ev'ry hour.
"All their afflictions, rightly understood,
"Are blessings; ev'ry wind will blow some good.
"Sure at their troubles saints would never grudge,
"Were sense deposed, and faith made the judge.
"Falls make them warier, amend their pace;
"When gifts puff up their hearts, and weaken grace.
"Could Satan see the issue, and th' event
"Of his temptations, he would scarcely tempt.
"Could saints but see what fruits their troubles bring,
"Amidst those troubles they would shout and sing.
"O sacred wisdom! who can but admire
"To see how thou dost save from fire, by fire!
"No doubt but saints in glory wond'ring stand
"At those strange methods few now understand.

CHAP. XXVIII.

Storms make discov'ry of the pilot's skill:
God's wisdom in affliction triumphs still.

OBSERVATION.

IN fair weather, when there is sea-room enough, then every common person can guide the ship;

the pilot may then lie down, and take his rest; but in great storms, and stress of weather, or when near the dangerous shore, then the most skilful pilot is put to it; then he shews the utmost of his art and skill, and yet sometimes all is too little. They are (as the scripture speaks) *at their wits end*, know not what to do more; but are forced to commit all to the mercy of God, and the seas.

APPLICATION.

In the storms and tempests of affliction and trouble, there are the most evident and full discoveries of the wisdom and power of our God: it is indeed continually active for his people in all conditions, Isa. xxvii. 3. "Lest any hurt it, I will "keep it night and day." Psal. cxxi. 4. "He that "keepeth Israel neither slumbereth nor sleepeth." His People's dangers are without intermission, therefore his preservations are so too. But now, when they come into the *strait* of affliction, and deadly dangers, which threaten like rocks on every side; now the wisdom of their God rides triumphantly and visibly upon the waves of that stormy sea; and this infinite wisdom is then especially discovered in these particulars:

1. In leaving them still somewhat in the lieu and room of those comforts that they are deprived of; so that they see God doth exchange their comforts, and that for the better; and this supports them. So John xiv. 1, 2, 3. Christ's bodily presence is removed, but the spirit was sent in the room of it, which was better.

2. In doubling their strength, as he doubles their burdens. It is observed that the saints have many times very strong and sweet consolation, a little before their greatest trials: and this is so ordinary, that commonly when they have had their extraordinary consolations from God, they have then looked for some eminent trial. The Lord appeared to Abraham, and sealed the covenant to him, and then put him upon that great trial of his faith. So the disciples, Luke xxiv. 49. It was commanded them that they "should tarry in Jerusalem, till "they were endowed with power from on high." The Lord knew what a hard providence they were like to have, and what great oppositions and difficulties they must encounter, in publishing the everlasting gospel to the world; and therefore first prepares and and endows them with power from on high, *viz.* with eminent measures of the gifts and graces of the Spirit; as faith, patience, self-denial, &c. So Paul had first his revelations, then his buffetings.

3. In coming in so opportunely in the time of their great distress, with relief and comfort, 1 Pet. iv. 14. "Then the Spirit of Glory and of God resteth on them." As that martyr cried out to his friend Austin, at the very stake, *He is come, he is come.*

4. In appointing and ordering the several kinds of afflictions to several saints; and alloting to every one, that very affliction, and no other, which is most suitable to his condition: which afflictions, like so many potions of physic, are prepared for that very malignant humour that predominates most in them. Peter's sin was self-confidence, God permits him to fall by denying Christ; which doubtless was sanctified to his good in that particular.

Hezekiah's sin was vain-glory, therefore spoilers are sent to take away his treasures.

5. In the duration of their troubles, they shall not ly always upon them, Psalm cxxv. 3. Our God is a God of judgment, Isa. xxx. 18. Knows the due time of removing it, and is therein punctual to a day, Rev. ii. 10.

REFLECTION.

If the wisdom of God do thus triumph, and glorify itself in the distresses of the saints, then why should I fear in the day of evil? Psalm xlix. 4. Why doth my heart faint at the fore-sight and apprehension of approaching trouble? Fear none of those things that thou shalt suffer, O my soul; if thy God will thus be with thee in the fire of water, thou canst not perish. Though I walk through the valley of the shadow of death, yet let me fear no evil, whilst my God is thus with me. Creatures cannot do what they please, his wisdom limits and over-rules them all, to gracious and sweet ends. If my God cast me into the furnace, to melt and try me, yet I shall not be consumed there; for he will sit by the furnace himself all the while I am in it, and curiously pry into it, observing when it hath done its work, and then will presently withdraw the fire. O my soul, bless and adore this God of wisdom! who himself will see the ordering of all thine afflictions, and not trust it in the hands of men or angels.

THE POEM.

"Though toft in greateft ftorms, I'll never fear,
"If Chrift will fit at th' helm to guide and fteer:
"Storms are the triumph of his fkill and art;
"He cannot clofe his eyes, nor change his heart.
"Wifdom and power ride upon the waves,
"And in the greateft danger helps and faves.
"From dangers it by dangers doth deliver,
"And wounds the devil out of his own quiver;
"It countermines his plots, and fo doth fpoil,
"And make his engines on himfelf recoil.
"It blunts the politician's reftlefs tool,
"And makes Ahitophel the verieft fool;
"It fhews us how our reafon us mifled,
"And if he had not, we had perifhed.
"Lord, to thy wifdom I will give the reins,
"And not with cares perplex and vex my brains."

CHAP. XXIX.

Things in the bottom are unfeen: no eye
Can trace God's paths, which in the deep do lie.

OBSERVATION.

THE ocean is fo deep, that no eye can difcover what lies in the bottom thereof. We ufe to say, proverbially, of a thing that is irrecoverably lost, it is as good it were cast into the sea. What lies there, lies obscure from all eyes, but the eye of God.

APPLICATION.

Thus are the judgments of God, and the ways of his providence, profound and unsearchable, Psal. xxxvi. 6. " Thy righteousness is like the great " mountains, thy judgments are a great deep ;" *(i. e.)* his providences are secret, obscure, and unfathomable ; but even then, and in those providences, his righteousness stands up like the great mountains, visible & apparent to every eye. Though the saints cannot see the one, yet they can clearly discern the other, Jer. xii. 1. Jeremiah was at a stand ; so was Job in the like case, Job xii. 7. So was Asaph, Psal. lxxiii. and Habbakuk, chap. i. 3. These wheels of providence are dreadful for their height, Ezek. i. 18. There be deep mysteries of providence, as well as of faith. It may be said of some of them, as of Paul's epistles, That they *are hard to be understood,* darkness and clouds are round about the throne of God : no man can say what will be the particular issue and event of some of his dispensations. Luther seemed to hear God say to him, when he was importunate to know his mind in some particular providence, *Deus sum non sequax*: I am a God not to be traced. Some providences, like Hebrew letters must be read backward, Psal. xcii. 7. Some providences pose men of the greatest parts and graces. " His way is in " the sea, his paths in the great waters, and his "foot-steps are not known," Pſal. lxxvii. 19. Who can trace foot-steps in the bottom of the ſea? "The Angels," Ezek. i. "have their hands un- "der their wings." The hand is either *ſymbolum roboris*. The ſymbol of ſtrength; or *inſtrumentatum operationis*, The inſtrument of action: where theſe hands are put forth, they work effectually, yea, but ſecretly, they are hid under their wings. There be ſome of God's works that are ſuch ſecrets, as that they may not be enquired into; they are to be believed and adored, but not pryed into, Rom. xi. 33. Others that may be enquired after, but yet are ſo profound, that few can underſtand them, Pſal. cxi. 2. "The works of the Lord are great; "ſought out of all thoſe that have pleaſure there- in." When we come to heaven, then all thoſe myſteries, as well in the works as in the words of God, will lie open to our view.

REFLECTION.

O then, why is my heart diſquieted, becauſe it cannot ſometimes diſcern the way of the Lord, and ſee the connection and dependance of his provi- dential diſpenſations? Why art thou ſo perplexed, O my ſoul, at the confuſions and diſorders that are in the world? I know that goodneſs and wiſdom ſits at the ſtern; and though the veſſel of the church be toſſed and diſtreſſed in ſtorms of trou- ble, yet it ſhall not periſh. Is it not enough for me, that God hath condeſcended ſo far, for my ſa- tisfaction, as to ſhew me plainly the ultimate and general iſſue of theſe myſterious providences, Eph. i. 22. Rom. viii. 28. unleſs I be able to take the height of every particular, shall I presume to call the God of heaven to account? Must he render a reason of his ways, and give an account of his matters to such a worm as I am? Be silent (O my soul) before the Lord, subscribe to his wisdom, and submit to his will, whatsoever he doth. However it be, yet God is good to Israel; the event will manifest it to be all over a design of love. I know not how to reconcile them to each other, or many of them to the promise; yet are they all harmonious betwixt themselves, and the certain means of accomplishing the promises. O what a favour is this, that in the midst of the greatest confusions in the world, God hath given such abundant security to his people, that it shall be well with them? Amos ix. 8. Eccles. viii. 12.

THE POEM.

"Lord! how stupendous, deep, and wonderful,
"Are all thy draughts of providence? So full
"Of puzzling intricacies, that they lie
"Beyond the ken of any mortal eye.
"*A wheel within a wheel*'s the scripture notion,
"And all those wheels transverse, and cross in motion.
"All creatures serve it in their place; yet so,
"As thousands of them know not what they do.
"At this or that, their aim they do direct;
"But neither this, nor that, is the effect:
"But something else they do not understand,
"Which sets all politicians at a stand.

"Deep counsels, at the birth, this hand doth break,
"And deeper things performeth by the weak.
"Men are, like horses, set at ev'ry stage,
"For providence to ride from age to age;
"Which, like a post, spurs on, and makes them run
"From stage, to stage, until their journey's done;
"Then take a fresh: but they the bus'ness know,
"No more than horses the post-letters do;
"Yet tho' it's work be not conceal'd from sight,
"'Twill be a glorious piece, when brought to light.

CHAP. XXX.

*Millions of men are sunk into the main;
But it shall not those dead always retain.*

OBSERVATION.

WHAT multitudes of men hath the sea devoured! thousands have made their graves in it. What numbers of men have been ingulfed together in sea-fights, or storms, or inundations, whereby whole towns have been swallowed up! certainly the dead which are there, are innumerable.

APPLICATION.

But though the sea has received so many thousand bodies of men into its devouring throat, yet it is not the absolute lord, or proprietor of them, but rather a steward intrusted with them, till the Lord require an account of them; and then it must deliver up all it hath received, even to a person. Rev. xx. 11, 12. "And I saw the dead, small and great, stand before God: And the books were opened; and another book was opened, which is the book of life; and the dead were judged out of those things which were written in the book, according to their works. And the sea gave up the dead which were in it."

The doctrine of the resurrection of the body, is a doctrine full of singular consolations to believers, 1 Cor. xv. and most clearly asserted in scripture, Acts xxvi. 8. Job xix. 25. 1 Cor. xv. &c. And it is well for us this point is so plainly revealed; because as it is a most comfortable truth to the people of God, so there is scarce any truth that lies under more prejudice, as to sense or reason, and is more difficult to receive, than this is. The Epicures and Stoics laughed *Paul* to scorn when he preached it to them, Acts xvii. 32. The Familists and Quakers at this day reject it as a fable. The Socinians say the same body shall not rise, but an ærial body. And, indeed, if men set up reason as the only judge of supernatural things, it is incredible to think, that a body should be restored, that hath been burnt to ashes, and those ashes scattered in the wind; as history tells us was frequently done by the bodies of the saints in *Dioclesian's* reign! or when drowned in the sea, and there devoured by several fishes, and those again devoured by others. But yet this is not to be objected to the almighty power of God, that gave them their first being: difficulties and impossibilities are for men, but not for him. "Why should it be thought a thing incredible with you, that God should raise the dead?" Acts xxvi. 8.

REFLECTION.

And muſt I riſe again, wherever my body falls at death? Then, Lord, how am I concerned to get union with Chriſt while I live? By virtue thereof only, my reſurrection can be made comfortable, and bleſſed to me. Ah! let my body lie where it will, in earth or ſea; let my bones be ſcattered, and fleſh devoured by worms or fiſh, I know thou canſt, and wilt re-unite my ſcattered parts; and in this body I muſt ſtand before thine awful tribunal, to receive according to what I have done therein, 2 Cor. v. 10. Thou that commandeſt me to ſtand forth among the nobleſt rank of creatures, when I had no being, and ſaweſt my ſubſtance, being yet imperfect, canſt as eaſily reduce me to that being again.

What though reaſon vote it impoſſible, and ſenſe incredible? Though all theſe difficulties and incumbrances grow upon my faith, yet I know my body is not loſt for ever; the ſound of thy laſt and dreadful trumpet, ſhall awaken me: and thy mighty power, to which all things are poſſible, ſhall bring me before thy bar.

O Lord, I know that I ſhall ſtand in that great aſſembly at the laſt day, when multitudes, multitudes, even all the ſons and daughters of Adam, ſhall appear together. O if I die Chriſtleſs, it were good for me that there were no reſurrection; for then thoſe eyes that have been windows of luſt, muſt behold Chriſt the Judge, not as a Redeemer, but as a Revenger. That tongue that hath vented ſo much of the filthineſs of my heart, will then be ſtruck ſpeechleſs before him; and this fleſh which I ſo pampered and provided for, condemned to everlasting flames. O my God, let me make sure work for such a day! if I now get real union with thy Son, I shall awake with singing out of the dust; and then, as thou saidst to *Jacob*, so to me, when I go down into the sea, or grave, Gen. xlvi. 3, 4. "Fear not to go down into the deep; for I will surely bring thee up again,"

THE POEM.

" It should not seem incredible to thee,
" That God should raise the dead in seas that be ;
" We see in winter, swallows, worms and flies
" Depriv'd of life, yet in the spring they rise.
" What tho' your bodies sev'ral fish devour,
" Object not that to the Almighty pow'r.
" Some chymists in their art are so exact,
" That from one herb they usually extract
" Four diff'rent elements; what think ye then,
" Can pose that God, who gave this skill to men?
" The gard'ner can distinguish thirty kinds
" Of seeds from one another, tho' he finds
" Them mix'd together in the self-same dish;
" Much more can God distinguish flesh from fish.
" They seem as lost, but they again must live;
" The sea's a steward, and stewards account must give.
" Look what you are, when in the ocean drown'd,
" The very same at judgment you'll be found.
" I would not care where my vile body lies,
" Were I assur'd it shou'd with comfort rise."

CHAP. XXXI.

The seaman's greatest danger's near the coast: When we are nearest heav'n, the danger's most.

OBSERVATION.

THOUGH seamen meet with violent storms, yet if they have sea room enough, they are not much dismayed: but if they find themselves near the shore, they look upon their condition as very dangerous: the sight of the shore is to them, (as Solomon speaks of the morning in another case) like the shadow of death, if not able to weather it. For one ship swallowed up in the ocean, many perish upon the coast.

APPLICATION.

The greatest straits and difficulties that many saints meet with in all their lives, is when they come nearest to heaven, and have almost finished their course. Heaven, indeed, is a glorious place, the spacious, and royal mansion of the great king; but *difficilia quae pulchra*; it hath a strait and narrow entrance, Luke xiii. 24. O the difficulty of arriving there! how many hard tugs in duty, what earnest contention and striving, even to an agony! as that word imports, Luke xiii. 24. Multitudes put forth, and by profession are bound for this *fair ha-*

ven: but of the multitudes that put out, how few do arrive there? A man may set out by a glorious profession, with much resolution, and continue long therein; he may offer very fair for it, and not be far from the kingdom of God, and yet not be able to enter at the last, Mat. vii. 22.

Yea, and many of those who are sincere in their profession, and do arrive at last, yet come to heaven (as I may say) by the gates of hell; and put in, as a poor weather-beaten vessel comes into the harbour, more like a wreck than a ship, neither mast nor sail left. The righteous themselves are scarcely saved, *(i. e.)* they are saved with very much difficulty. They have not all an *abundant entrance*, as the apostle speaks, 2 Pet. i. 11.

"Some persons (as one well notes) are *afar off*, Eph. ii. 23. *(i. e.)* touched with no care of religion: some come near, but never enter, as semi-converts. See Matth. xii. 34. Others enter, but with great difficulty, they are saved as by fire, 1 Cor. iii. 13. Make an hard shift. But then there are some that go in with full sail before the wind, and have an abundant entrance: they go triumphing out of the world." Ah! when we come into the narrow channel, at the very point of entrance into life, the soul is then in the most serious frame; all things look with a new face; conscience scans our evidence most critically; then, also, Satan falls upon us, and makes his sorest assults, and batteries. It is the last encounter; if they escape him now, they are gone out of his reach for ever: and if he cannot hinder their salvation, yet if he can but cloud their evening, and make them go groaning and howling out of the world, he reaches another end by it, even to confirm and prejudice the wicked and weaken the hands of others that are looking towards religion.

REFLECTION.

If this be so, how inevitable is my perdition, may the careless soul say? If they that strive so much, and go so far, yet perish at last; and if the righteous themselves are scarcely saved; then where shall such an ungodly creature as I appear? O Lord! if they that have made religion their business, and have been many years pursuing a work of mortification, have gone mourning after the Lord Jesus, and walked humbly with God; yet if some of these have such an hard tug at last, then what will become of such a vain, sensual, careless, flesh-pleasing wretch as I have been?

Again; Do saints find it so strait an entrance? Then, though I have well grounded hopes of safe arrival at last; yet let me look to it, that I do not increase the difficulty. Ah! they are the things that are now done, or omitted, that put conscience into such an agony then; for then it comes to review the life with the most serious eye. O let me not stick my death bed full of thorns, against I come to lie down upon it. O that I may turn to the wall, in that hour, as *Hezekiah* did, 2 Kings xx. 2, 3. and say, "Remember now, O Lord, how I have walked before thee in truth, and with a perfect heart," &c.

THE POEM.

"After a tedious passage, saints descry
"The glorious shore, salvation being nigh:
"Death's long boat's launch'd, ready to set ashore
"Their panting souls. O how they tug at oar,

"Longing to be at rest! but then they find
"The hardest tug of all is yet behind.
"Just at the harbour's mouth they see the wreck
"Of souls there cast away, and driven back.
"A world of dang'rous rocks before it lie;
"The harbour's barr'd, and now the winds blow high:
"Thoughts now arise, fears multiply apace;
"All things about them have another face.
"Life blazes, just like an expiring light,
"The soul's upon the lip prepar'd for flight.
"Death, till the resurrection, tears and rends,
"Out of each other's arms, two parting friends,
"The soul and body. Ah! but more than so,
"The devil falls upon them e're they go,
"With new temptations, back'd with all his pow'r,
"And scruples, kept on purpose for that hour.
"This is the last encounter, now, or never;
"If he succeedeth now, they're gone for ever.
"Thus in they put, with hardship at the last,
"As ships out of a storm, nor sail, nor mast:
"Yet some go in before a wind, and have
"Their streamer of assurance flying brave.
"Lord, give me easier entrance; if thou please;
"Or if I may not there arrive with ease,
"Yet I beseech thee, set me safe a-shore;
"Tho' stormy winds at harbour's mouth should roar.

CHAP. XXXII.

*How glad are seamen when they make the shore?
And saints, no less, when all their danger's o'er.*

OBSERVATION.

WHAT joy is there among seamen, when at last, after a tedious and dangerous voyage, they descry land, and see the desired haven before them? Then they turn out of their loathed cabins, and come upon open deck with much joy. Psalm cvii. 30. "Then they are glad, because they be quiet: So he bringeth them to their desired haven." Now they can reflect, with comfort, upon the many dangers they have past, *Olim haec meminisse juvabit*; it is sweet to recount them.

APPLICATION.

But O what a transcendant joy, yea, ravishing, will over-run the hearts of saints, when, after so many conflicts, temptations, and afflictions, they arrive in glory, and are harboured in heaven, where they shall rest forever! 2 Thess. i. 7. The scripture saith, "They shall sing the song of Moses, and of the Lamb," Rev. xv. 3. The song of Moses was a triumphant song, composed for the celebration of that glorious deliverance at the red sea. The saints are now fluctuating upon a troublesome and tempestuous sea; their hearts sometimes ready to sink, and die within them, at the apprehension of so many and great dangers and difficulties. Many a hard storm they ride out, and many straits and troubles they here encounter with, but at last they arrive at their desired and long expected haven, and then heaven rings and resounds with their joyful acclamations. And how can it be otherwise, when as soon as ever they set foot upon that glorious shore, Christ himself meets and receives them, with a "Come ye blessed of my Father," Matth. xxv. 34. O joyful voice! O much desired word!

faith Paraeus, what tribulation would not a man undergo for his word's fake!

Besides, then they are perfectly freed from all evils, whether of fin or fuffering, and perfectly filled with all defired good. Now they fhall join with that great affembly, in the high praifes of God. O what a day will this be! if, faid a worthy divine, Diagoras died away with an excefs of joy, whilft he embraced his three fons that were crowned as victors in the Olympic games in one day: and good old Simeon, when he faw Chrift but in a body fubject to the infirmities of our nature, cried out, "Now let thy fervant depart in peace;" what unfpeakable joy will it be to the faints, to behold Chrift in his glory, and fee their godly relations alfo (to whofe converfion, perhaps, they have been inftrumental) all crowned, in one day, with everlafting diadems of blifs! and if the ftars did, as Ignatus faith, make a choir, as it were, about that ftar, that appeared at Chrift's incarnation, and there is fuch joy in heaven at the converfion of a finner; no wonder, then, the morning ftars fing together, and the fons of God fhout for joy, when the general affembly meet in heaven: O how will the arches of heaven ring, and echo, when the high praifes of God fhall be in the mouth of fuch a congregation! then fhall the faints be joyful in glory, and fing aloud upon their beds of everlafting reft.

REFLECTION.

And is there fuch a day approaching for the fons of God, indeed! and have I [*authority*] to call myself one of the number! John i. 12. O then let me not droop at present difficulties, nor hang down my hands when I meet with hardships in the way. O my soul, what a joyful day will this be! for at present we are tossed upon an ocean of troubles, fears, and temptations; but these will make heaven the sweeter.

Chear up, then, O my soul, thy salvation is now nearer than when thou first believedst, Rom. xiii. 11. and it will not now be long e're I receive the end of my faith, 1 Pet. i. 9. and then it will be sweet to reflect even upon these hardships in the way. Yet a few days more, and then comes that blessed day thou hast so long waited and panted for. Oppose the glory of that day, O my soul, to thy present abasures and sufferings, as blessed Paul did, Rom. i. 18. and thou shalt see how it will shrink them all up to nothing; oppose the inheritance thou shalt receive in that day, to thy losses for Christ now; and see how joyfully it will make thee bear them, Heb. x. 34. oppose the honor that will be put upon thee in that day, to thy present reproaches, and see how easy it will make them to thee, 1 Cor. iv. 5. What condition can I be in, wherein the believing thoughts of this blessed day cannot relieve me?

Am I poor, here is that which answers poverty. Jam. iii. 5. "Hearken, my beloved brethren, "hath not God chosen the poor of this world, "rich in faith, and heirs of the kingdom?"

Am I tempted? here is relief against that, Rev. xii. 16. "Now is come salvation and strength; "for the accuser of our brethren is cast down," &c.

Am I deserted? here is a remedy for that too, Rev. xxii. 5. "And there shall be no night

" there," &c. Come then, my soul, let us enter upon our inheritance by degrees, and begin the life of heaven upon earth.

THE POEM.

" When Solomon in Israel first was king,
" Heaven's arches, earth's foundation seem'd to ring
" With joyful exclamations ? how much more
" Will heav'n resound, when saints are come ashore !
" How will the ravish'd souls transported be,
" At the first glimpse of Christ ! whom they shall see
" In all his glory ; and shall live and move,
" Like salamandors, in the fire of love.
" A flood of tears convey'd them to the gate
" Where endless joys receiv'd them.   Now the date
" Of all their sorrows's out ; henceforth they walk
" In robes of glory.   Now there's no more talk
" Of fears, temptations, of that snare, or this :
" No serpent in that paradise doth hiss.
" No more desertions, troubled thoughts, or tears ;
" Christ's full enjoyment supersedes those fears.
" Delights of princes are all but toys
" To these delights, these are transcendent joys,
" The joys of Christ himself ; of what they are,
" An Angel's tongue wou'd stammer to declare.
" Were our conceptions clear, did their tongue go
" Unto their Ela, yet the note's too low.
" What ! paint the sun too bright ! it cannot be ;
" Sure heaven suffers no hyperbole.
" My thoughts are swallow'd up, my muse doth tire,
" And bangs her wings, conception soars no higher.
" Give me a place among thy children there,
" Altho' I ly with them in dungeon here.

A CONCLUDING SPEECH.

I HAVE now done, and am looking to heaven for a blessing upon these weak labours; what use you will make of them, I know not, but this I know, that the day is coming, when God will reckon with you for this, and all other helps and means afforded to you: and if it be not improved by you, be sure it will be produced as a witness against you. Sirs, I beg you, in the name of Christ, before whom both you and I must shortly appear, that you receive not these things in vain. Did I know what other lawful means to use that might reach your hearts, they should not be in vain to you; but I cannot do God's part of the work, nor your's: only I request you all, both masters, common men, and all others into whose hands this shall come, that you will lay to heart what you read; pray unto him that hath the key of the house of David, that openeth and no man shutteth, to open your hearts to give entertainment to these truths. Alas! if you apply it not to yourselves, I have laboured to no purpose; the pen of the scribe is in vain: but God may make such an application of them, in one storm or another, as may make your heart to tremble. O sirs! when death and eternity look you in the face, conscience may reflect upon these things to your horror and amazement, and make you cry out, as Prov. v. 12, 13. " How have I " hated knowledge, and my heart despised reproof!

"and have not obeyed the voice of my teacher, "nor inclined my ears to them that instructed "me?" And O what a dreadful shriek will such souls give, when the Lord opens their eyes to see that misery that they are here warned of. But if the Lord shall bless these things, to your conversion, then we may say to you, as Moses did to Zebulun, the mariners tribe, Deut. xxxiii. 12. "Rejoice "Zebulun in thy going out." The Lord will be with you, which way soever you turn yourselves; and being in the bosom of the covenant, you are safe in the midst of all dangers. O thou, that art the Father of spirits, that formedst and canst easily reform the heart, open thou the blind eye, unstop the deaf ear, let the world take hold upon the heart. If thou wilt but say the word, these weak labours shall prosper, to bring home many lost souls unto thee.

A M E N.

EDMUND M. BLUNT,

Printer & Book-binder,

AT THE

Newburyport Book-Store,

STATE-STREET,

(Five Doors below Mr. DAVENPORT's Tavern,)

KEEPS CONSTANTLY FOR SALE,

A LARGE AND EXTENSIVE COLLECTION OF

BOOKS

IN THE DIFFERENT

BRANCHES OF LITERATURE;

ALSO,

BIBLES of all kinds and prices—Testaments—Watt's Psalms and Hymns—Perry's, Webster's, and Dilworth's Spelling Books and Primers, by the Groce, Dozen or Single—Ainsworth's and Young's Latin Dictionaries—Greek Lexicons, Testaments and Grammars—Clark's Eutropius, Erasmus, and Introduction to making of Latin, Davidson's Virgil—Cicero's Orations, with and without Translations—Perry's and Entick's Pocket Dictionaries—Pike's Arithmetic; Fenning's Ditto—Moore's Practical Navigator—Seaman's daily assistant—Ship Master's Assistant—Mariners Compass—With a Variety of others including all the Books generally used at Colleges, Academies, Schools, &c. at the lowest prices.

LIKEWISE,

A LARGE ASSORTMENT OF

STATIONARY,

OF EVERY KIND.

Jan. 1797.

www.ingramcontent.com/pod-product-compliance
Lightning Source LLC
Chambersburg PA
CBHW030303170426
43202CB00009B/856